PARACHUTES and RIBBONS and SCARVES, OH MY!

LISTENING LESSONS WITH MOVEMENT PROPS

ARTIE ALMEIDA

Editors: Jeanette Morgan and Kris Kropff
Cover Design: Kate Kimble
Book Design: WordStreamCopy
Musical recordings under license from Naxos of America, Inc. www.Naxos.com 2010 HNH International Ltd. All rights reserved. Unlawful duplication, broadcast or performance of the audio is prohibited by applicable law.

© 2011 Heritage Music Press, a division of The Lorenz Corporation, and its licensors. All rights reserved.

Heritage Music Press
A division of The Lorenz Corporation
PO Box 802
Dayton OH 45401

www.lorenz.com

Printed in the United States of America.

ISBN: 978-1-4291-2104-0

Contents

	Track	Page
Preface		4
Tips and Suggestions		6

"Finale" to the Overture from William Tell
	Track	Page
Guided Listing with Non-pitched Percussion	1	7
Form Chart		10
Guided Listening with Parachute Play	1	11
Flashlight Activity	1	15

The Syncopated Clock
	Track	Page
Moving with Scarves	2–3	19
Form Chart		21
Vocabulary Flash Cards		22

The Wild Horseman
	Track	Page
Giddy-Up! A Stick-Horse Activity	4	27
Form Chart		29

"Galop" from The Comedians
	Track	Page
A Ribbon Streamer Movement Activity	5	30
Form Chart		32

"March" from The Nutcracker
	Track	Page
A Form Lesson Activated with Plastic Plates	6	34
Form Chart		37
A Form Lesson Activated with Large Plastic Candy Canes	6	38
A Form Lesson Activated with a Stretchy Band	6	41

"Trepak (Russian Dance)" from The Nutcracker
	Track	Page
A Form Lesson Activated with Ribbon Wands	7	43
Form Chart		45
A Form Lesson Activated with Parachute Play	7	46

"Viennese Musical Clock" from Háry János Suite
	Track	Page
Movement with Large Scarves	8	48
Form Chart		50
Creative Movement Groups	8	52

Rondo Alla Turca
	Track	Page
Guided Listening with Student Responder Packs	9	55
Form Chart		57
Mozart Scramble Info Sheet		58
Animal Responders		59

The Stars and Stripes Forever
	Track	Page
Flag Routine	10	64
Form Chart		67
Picture of John Philip Sousa		68

	Track	Page

EL CAPITAN
A Plastic Cup Routine.. 11 70
   Form Chart...73
   Picture of El Capitan...74

"IN THE HALL OF THE MOUNTAIN KING" FROM PEER GYNT SUITE NO. 1
Experiencing Tempo and Dynamics with Kickballs and Guiros 12 76
   Vocabulary Flash Cards 79

FAMILY MUSICAL MOMENTS

These lesssons offer a wonderful opportunity to build a school/home/family connection! I do this by sending home a small slip of paper with each child about the experience. These Family Musical Moment notes encourage families to share the experience by listening to a piece of music together. (Some of my students will even teach their families the movement routines!)

We have included a page of Family Musical Moment notes for each lesson in the download files so you can easily print as many as you need to serve your student population. You'll also find these reproducibles throughout the resource on the pages listed below should you prefer to photocopy them.

"Finale" to the Overture from *William Tell*
   Guided Listing with Non-pitched Percussion 9
   Guided Listening with Parachute Play 14
   Flashlight Activity 18
The Syncopated Clock 26
The Wild Horseman 28
"Galop" from *The Comedians* 33
"March" from *The Nutcracker*
   A Form Lesson Activated with Plastic Plates..36
   A Form Lesson Activated with Large Plastic Candy Canes..40
   A Form Lesson Activated with a Stretchy Band..42
"Trepak (Russian Dance)" from *The Nutcracker*
   A Form Lesson Activated with Ribbon Wands..44
   A Form Lesson Activated with Parachute Play 47
"Viennese Musical Clock" from *Háry János Suite*
   Movement with Large Scarves..51
   Creative Movement Groups 54
Rondo Alla Turca 63
The Stars and Stripes Forever..69
El Capitan 75
"In the Hall of the Mountain King" from *Peer Gynt Suite No. 1* 78

Preface

Heavy Academics, Delivered Joyfully

Welcome to the wonderful world of guided listening with movement and props, a world where we can help our students develop excellent ears while they are joyfully responding to some of the greatest classical pieces of all time! You're going to love teaching these activities and your students will have a blast while learning about musical elements, composers, and great musical works. It's a win-win situation for teachers and students alike.

My personal theme in the music classroom is, "Heavy Academics, Delivered Joyfully." These lessons certainly fit that bill and are favorites in my classroom at Bear Lake Elementary. I hope you and your students feel the same way!

Learn to Listen and Listen to Learn

Guided-listening lessons help grow young music analysts by developing critical listeners who have been exposed to a large variety of music that, in all likelihood, they would never have discovered on their own. These young music analysts notice musical details and can describe them with appropriate music vocabulary *and* they become invested in those pieces, because they were presented in fun and age-appropriate ways.

I was blessed with a mother who played an enormous variety of music in our home. I grew up hearing great music every single day: classical, jazz, folk, ethnic, and pop. That certainly empowered me as I became a performer in later years.

Why Add Movement Props?

My approach to lesson planning has always been to provide children with the opportunity to sing, play, listen, and move every time they enter my room. Years ago, when I began adding a lot of movement to my program, I had to deal with a number of behavior issues in my very large, and active, classes. Eventually, I discovered that the power of a prop is not to be underestimated.

While still offering a lot of free- and creative-movement opportunities, I began to collect a variety of props that I hoped would be appealing to my students while allowing me to fill their ears with loads of great music. When I saw the joyful response from the children, I was hooked. Plus, put props in the hands of those children with very short attention spans and you now have 10–12 minutes of focused teaching time. Amazing!

A Note about the Videos

It was my dream to offer you a book that included all of the lessons, all of the recordings you need for those lessons, and video footage of "real kids" doing the movement routines. I'm thrilled to see it come to fruition!

Now, these video demos are not polished performances. Each video is a first take and the group of students is a diverse cross section of my school population. They stayed after school, I prepped the lessons, and then we passed out the props and shot the video. Some of the lessons were experienced by students this year in their grade level, while many of the lessons were brand new to them the days we filmed.

During the filming all children put forth a fabulous effort! This was really a family affair, with lots of little brothers and sisters staying after school with their siblings, and they were thrilled to jump in and join us in the lessons. However, due to the large spread of grade levels, you'll see some children who "get it" while others are struggling a little.

It greatly amused me to see how much fun the intermediate-aged children had while demonstrating the lessons that I designed for much younger students. The fifth graders *loved* riding the stick horses and candy-cane critters (so much so that I am thinking of placing some of those lessons into older grade levels next year!).

Thank you! Thank you! Thank you!

I am indebted to many folks for this project. My editor Jeanette Morgan; my brain-storming-buddies Katie Miller, Stephen Nelson, and Bonnie Shea; and the good folks at Lorenz.

Brava! Brava! to Mrs. Edstrom, our Camerawoman/Super Mom from Bear Lake. Her five children are a delight to teach, and I will be eternally grateful for all the hours she devoted to our project. She would zoom over to Bear Lake after teaching all day at the local college, shoot video for two hours, then gather her kiddos and head home to make dinner and begin the evening's homework, etc. My hat is off to her!

And most of all, many thanks to my wonderful Bear Lake students who are featured in the videos. They came each day after long hours at school, and some days we filmed after finishing our hour-long ensemble rehearsal. What troopers!

I asked a lot of children to be part of the filming, assuming that most days only a portion of them would be available. Well, these Bear Lake parents are dedicated and most of the children came most of the time! It is a large group in the videos, almost as large as my daily music classes—all the better to give you a very good idea of how these activities will *really* look in your classroom.

As I previewed the videos I often found myself with tears in my eyes, watching each child's personality shine through these activities. When I'm teaching I am focused on calling the cues, monitoring the behavior, and creating a musical setting. Often I don't really see the details of what's going on. What fun it was to sit back, relax, and watch my children respond to some of my favorite musical works. I love you, my little bear cubs!

The Bear Lake VidKids

Jonathan A.	Devyn N.	Daniel S.
Ashley A.	Paige N.	Julia S. (the second Julia)
Angelina B.	Abigail P.	Alicia S.
Brittany B.	Madison R.	Ashley T.
Deenah B.	Essence S.	Bobby W.
Kiana B.	Julia S.	Darin W.
Nick B.		
Shaun B.		
Thomas B.		
Walker D.		
Kristofer E.		
Niklas E.		
Camille G.		
Tammy G.		
Danyele H.		
Jessica H.		
Madison H.		
Nicole M.		

Tips and Suggestions

Repetition, Repetition, Repetition

I often use a guided-listening piece as Entrance Music or Exit Music during the week I'm presenting that lesson, or in lessons that come before or after the movement instruction. The more times the children hear the piece, the more they love it and feel ownership of the work. (Research shows that the music we learn in childhood we love forever.)

You'll also notice that I embed my composer information within the lessons. Because I'm on a six-day rotation at Bear Lake, I've had to cut some things from my yearly curriculum. I no longer do a Composer Unit, for example. Instead I include Five Fun Facts, Ten Tidbits, Pictures, Scrambled Info, etc. into the listening lessons, helping the students get to know the composers.

Selecting Grade Levels

These movement lessons work well across numerous grade levels. I usually divide them amongst my K–5 classes, but you could easily teach all of these plans to all of your elementary-aged children. Additionally, there are a number of lessons that work with middle-school-aged children, and I have even done the flashlight painting activity with high school band students!

One approach that has been particularly effective for me is to use the same piece of music in different ways with different props. Children love revisiting a lesson first presented in the primary grades in their intermediate years, but this time with a new activity and prop. I get lesson requests all of the time from brothers and sisters who were told about a prop activity at home and wish for me to teach it to *their* class. Gotta love that!

School/Home/Family Connections

I seek out every opportunity for school/home/family connections and have included my Family Musical Moment guided-listening notes throughout this resource (see page 3 for a list of where each can be found). They are also available in the printable resources online. I photocopy these strips on brightly colored paper and send them home with children after a listening lesson. Many of my students then listen to the piece of music at home and share it with their family, often teaching the movement routine as well. Numerous parents at my school have spoken to me about how they are building a family music library thanks to the Family Musical Moment notes.

Accessing the Audio, Visual, and Printable Resources

For your convenience, all of the visuals and teaching aids presented in this text are available in color (for projection) and black and white (for printing). To access the audio, visual, and printable resources:

Go to
www.lorenz.com/resources/parachutes
Password: CZV9C3BC

Suggested Grade Levels: K–5

GUIDED LISTENING WITH NON-PITCHED PERCUSSION

"Finale" to the Overture from *William Tell*

By Gioachino Rossini (1792–1868)

Focus on form by adding non-pitched percussion to this favorite.

MATERIALS

Recording—Track 1
Form Chart (see page 10)
Jingle bell clusters, Maracas, Hand drums
Three Hula Hoops (optional)

PREPARATION

Set up three instrument stations for the non-pitched percussion: jingle bells, maracas, and hand drums. The hula hoops are a great organizational tool for the stations: place three hula hoops on the floor and put all of the maracas (or hand drums, etc.) inside one of the hoops. Be sure to place enough instruments in each hoop to service one third of your class.

Before teaching this lesson, you'll want to practice this piece a number of times to feel comfortable with the complex form. Accurate entrances and cut-offs are of great importance to the success of the activity. The coda is lengthy and you will need to practice cueing the final roll of the instruments.

INSTRUCTIONAL STEPS

1. Consider telling the folk legend of William Tell, a Swiss folk hero. The characters include the big, bad sheriff, the imprisoned archer, and the desperate son. Of course, there's also the famous scene of Poppa Tell shooting an apple off his son's head, without moving a hair. There are numerous versions of the story available in print and online.

2. Display the Form Chart for this piece, and discuss it with the children. Be sure to address the following vocabulary words as you discuss the chart:

    a. Introduction

    b. Interlude

    c. Coda

    d. Conductor

    e. Steady Beat

3. Explain that today's guided-listening activity will give the students a chance to play in a non-pitched percussion ensemble, under the direction of a very famous conductor—you! Demonstrate proper playing technique for each of the three instruments, and tell the students that the jingle bells will be

playing during all of the A Sections, maracas during the B Sections, and the hand drums during the C Sections. No one should play during the D Section. Let the students know that they all play together during the Coda.

4. Explain that you, as their conductor, will help to cue them to play at the appropriate times, and that the professional orchestra they will hear on the recording was also watching a conductor's cues as they recorded this famous piece.

5. Assign the students to their stations and ask them to warm-up the instruments until you give a cut-off signal. After they are warmed up, lead the students through some starts and stops, as well as playing along to the conductor's beat. While I sometimes conduct with a regular $\frac{4}{4}$ conducting pattern, many times throughout this activity, I actually clap the beat for the students to follow. Use whichever technique works best for you. (This decision is often determined by the students' age and experience level.)

6. Perform the piece by conducting or clapping the steady beat throughout the piece, using the following guidelines and referencing the Form Chart visual as needed:

    a. Have students begin in some sort of a resting position.

    b. Give a cue for "instruments up and ready." (Sometimes I like to do the clichéd, but fun, tap on the music stand and snap arms up into ready position.)

    c. Start the recording. Instruments stay up and ready during the Introduction. Make eye contact with the A Section players just before they begin.

    d. Give a strong entrance cue for your A Section players and conduct or clap the beat for them throughout the section. Give a quick cut-off for them at the end and turn quickly to the B Section players.

    e. Bring the B Section players in and make bold conducting or clapping motions to help them respond appropriately to this powerful melody. Give a clear cut-off to the B Section players and, as the Interlude plays, move your eyes and body back toward the A Section players.

    f. Conduct the A Section players once more, putting the C Section players on alert with an eye signal.

    g. Conduct the C Section with large motions for the first two measures and smaller motions for the following two. Repeat.

    h. Do not conduct the D Section, but rather keep children in an alert position as they listen.

    i. Conduct the C Section players once again.

    j. Quickly move into position to conduct the B Section. Give a good cut-off as the B Section transitions into the Interlude. Make eye contact with your A Section players and move toward them.

"Finale" to the Overture from William Tell

k. Conduct the last A Section, taking a moment to tell the children that everyone should prepare for the Coda.

l. During the Coda, conduct the steady beat most of the time, with some slower beats being played as dictated by the music. Finish with a grand, *fortissimo* roll and give an artistic cut-off. Ask the players to take a bow and acknowledge the wild applause of the audience.

7. In a subsequent lesson, assign students to a different instrument station and repeat the experience.

Tour with this all-time favorite by taking your students to the school cafeteria, front office, kindergarten rooms, special education classrooms, etc. and performing for the other children. It's sure to be a big hit, with cheers of "Bravo! Brava!" ringing out! So that the cheers can continue at home, give each student a Family Musical Moment note as they leave so they can find the music online or on a recording.

Activity at a Glance

Introduction	Ready position
A Section	Jingle bells
B Section	Maracas
Interlude	Prepare for A
A Section	Jingle bells
C Section	Hand drums
D Section	Listen
C Section	Hand drums
B Section	Maracas
Interlude	Prepare for A
A Section	Jingle bells
Coda	Everyone

Family Musical Moment

Today in music class we listened to the "Finale" from the *William Tell Overture* composed by Gioachino Rossini. We activated the experience with classroom percussion instruments. The instructional focus included Steady Beat and Form. Share a musical moment with your child by listening to this exciting piece of music together.

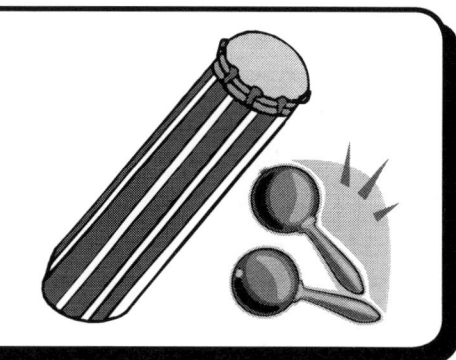

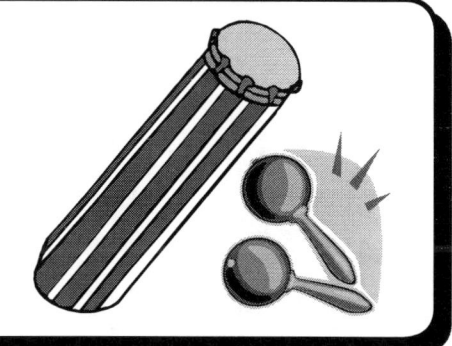

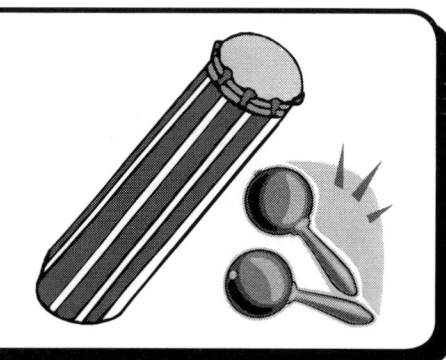

Family Musical Moment

Today in music class we listened to the "Finale" from the *William Tell Overture* composed by Gioachino Rossini. We activated the experience with classroom percussion instruments. The instructional focus included Steady Beat and Form. Share a musical moment with your child by listening to this exciting piece of music together.

Family Musical Moment

Today in music class we listened to the "Finale" from the *William Tell Overture* composed by Gioachino Rossini. We activated the experience with classroom percussion instruments. The instructional focus included Steady Beat and Form. Share a musical moment with your child by listening to this exciting piece of music together.

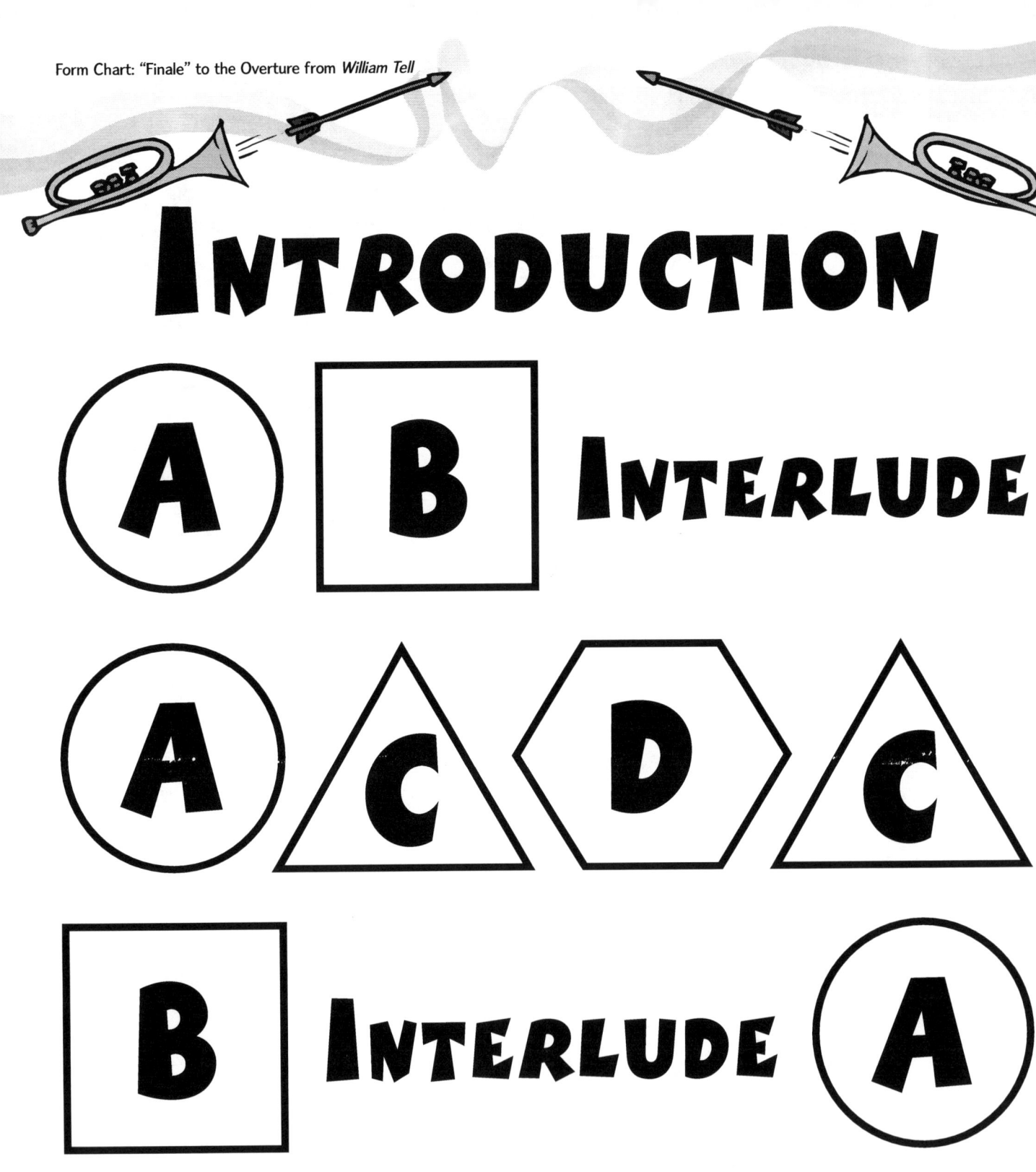

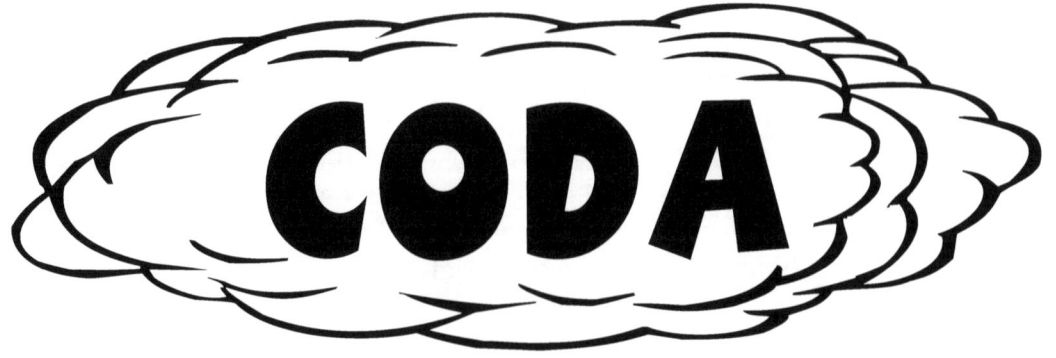

Form Chart: "Finale" to the Overture from *William Tell*

Introduction

(A) [B] Interlude

(A) △C △D △C

[B] Interlude (A)

CODA

The original purchaser of *Parachutes and Ribbons and Scarves, Oh My!* (30/2626H) by Artie Almeida has permission to reproduce this page for use in his or her classroom setting. © 2011 Heritage Music Press, a division of The Lorenz Corporation.

Suggested Grade Levels: 2–5

GUIDED LISTENING WITH PARACHUTE PLAY

"Finale" to the Overture from *William Tell*

By Gioachino Rossini (1792–1868)

Focus on form and steady beat with this parachute routine.

MATERIALS

Recording—Track 1
Form Chart (see page 10)
Parachute*

PREPARATION

Discuss the form of the piece and, if applicable, the previous activity with non-pitched percussion instruments. Because cueing (calling out) accurate entrances and section changes are of great importance to the success of the activity, before teaching this lesson you'll want to practice this piece a number of times to feel comfortable with its complex form.

INSTRUCTIONAL STEPS

1. Share or review the folk legend of William Tell.

2. Display the Form Chart for this piece (see page 10) and discuss it with the children. Vocabulary words to address include:

    a. Introduction

    b. Interlude

    c. Coda

    d. Conductor

    e. Steady Beat

3. Discuss, interpret, then practice the following movements:

    a. *Trotting* (one of the gaits that a horse uses) is like a jogging motion. Knees come up pretty high and the feet come well off the floor.

    b. *Ripples and Waves* means to shake the parachute to the beat. These shakes are not very large.

    c. *Mushrooms* are created by moving the parachute quickly up above the head, then bringing the arms down slowly, creating a mushroom shape as the parachute descends. This move lasts for four measures and is then repeated, allowing for two mushrooms to fit into the C Section.

---

* I use a 12' parachute because of the limited space in my room. If you have large classes consider doing this lesson outside or in a gymnasium with a 20' parachute. If you do not have a parachute, check with your physical education department. They may have one.

11

d. *The Washing Machine* is created by holding the parachute at waist height and moving it back and forth with the arms, simulating the agitator in some washing machines. (I have no idea what I'm going to call this move when washing machines with agitators become nothing more than a relic of the old days!)

4. Establish and discuss safety rules for the parachute lesson. It is essential that the children are careful of any instruments that may be in the music room while they are moving. Care needs to be taken not to tear the parachute. Let the children know that the parachute belongs to all of the students at the school, and that children abusing the prop will be removed from the activity. If the children are overly aggressive with some of the parachute maneuvers they can hurt other children's arms. Children who are out of control during the routine should be removed.

5. Emphasize the fact that no talking is allowed during guided-listening activities, even very exciting ones like this. My students get so excited when the parachute first comes out that they are chatty and exuberant. Give them some time to celebrate, then remind them that the only reason we are using the parachute today is to interpret and demonstrate what we hear in the music. Explain that while the physical education coach uses the parachute for a cardiac workout and to develop arm strength, we are going to be exercising our ears with the 'chute! If students are talking and the music cannot be clearly heard, then the activity is pointless.

6. Direct the students to stand up and make a circle with everyone distributed evenly around the circle. If there are gaps in the circle, they must be closed before the parachute is picked up. Place the parachute in the center of the circle and instruct the children to wait for your direction to pick it up. If you value your life, step out of the circle before you give this direction!

7. Perform the routine calling cues throughout the piece. Be sure to speak your cues early (as one section is ending) so that the students can start each subsequent section on time. Remember that the form is: Introduction/AB/Interlude/ACDCB/Interlude/A/Coda. Refer your students to the Form Chart again, before you begin the movement activity.

    Introduction: Listen to the introduction with students holding the parachute in their left hands, while facing to their right in the circle.

    A Section: Students hold the parachute in their left hands and trot to the right in a circle, keeping the parachute pulled tight and flat. For your older children, consider turning to trot in the other direction halfway through the A Section.

    B Section: Students face the center and shake the parachute to the beat, creating *Ripples and Waves*. Be ready for the hoots and hollers of joy. Kiddos of all ages love this part of the music!

    Interlude: Turn back to the right and wait for the A Section to return.

    A Section: Same as above.

    C Section: Facing the center, have all students quickly lift the parachute above their heads, then bring their arms down slowly, creating a mushroom shape as the parachute descends. This move lasts for four measures and is then repeated, giving you two mushrooms in the C Section.

    D Section: Have your students face the center, hold the parachute at waist height and do *The Washing Machine*, moving the parachute back and forth (right then left) with the arms. I always instruct my students to start to

"Finale" to the Overture from William Tell

their right, but if you've taught for any length of time, you understand that this can be a lesson in futility. If the parachute is being pulled in two different directions, don't panic—this usually corrects itself midway through the D Section.

C Section: Same as above.

B Section: Same as above.

Interlude: Same as above.

A Section: Same as above.

Coda: Start doing *Ripples and Waves* (lots and lots of them!) to the quarter-note beat but listen for the four big, bombastic slower notes and match the slower rhythm with the movement. Immediately follow the four big, slower shakes with a *Mushroom*. Then repeat that sequence of fast shakes, four slow shakes, and a *Mushroom*. Next, change to small *Ripples and Waves* and pause when the music pauses for a beat or two.

Continue on the wild ride to the end with fast shakes, then eight big, slower shakes matching the accents in the music. Finally, have the students stop moving the parachute completely, bend over slightly, and listen for the grand finale. On the final three notes of the piece, call out "One, two, toss!" The students should then toss the parachute toward the ceiling. If all of the children release the parachute together, it will stick to the ceiling. This is the children's favorite part and they love seeing what happens next. The parachute will usually spiral down in a hurry to the center of the circle or float away across the room like a huge jellyfish, sometimes landing on one of the children.

To keep this ending from becoming chaotic, instruct the children (before you begin the parachute game) that they are not to move their feet from where they stand during the Coda. All children must freeze the second the parachute is tossed into the air. If the parachute lands on them, they must stand there covered like a little ghost, until you retrieve it. Additionally, if the parachute floats away like a jellyfish, they are not allowed to chase it, but must just stand still and enjoy the show. (One day when I presented this lesson the parachute floated over by the front door and landed right on the second-grade teacher who was waiting to pick up her class. The kids and I howled with laughter. Oh, how I wish I had a video of that moment!)

As an instructor, be sure to practice the Coda a number of times on your own before you teach this to children. It is very intense and will be the most passionate part of the lesson if done correctly.

8. The students will leave your room begging for more, and will want to download the piece as soon as they get home. Give them a Family Musical Moment note as they leave so they can find the music online or on a recording (see page 14).

Activity at a Glance

Introduction	Listening
A Section	Trotting
B Section	*Ripples and Waves*
Interlude	Prepare for A
A Section	Trotting
C Section	*Mushrooms*
D Section	*The Washing Machine*
C Section	*Mushrooms*
B Section	*Ripples and Waves*
Interlude	Prepare for A
A Section	Trotting
Coda	*Ripples and Waves*

FAMILY MUSICAL MOMENT

Today in music class we listened to the "Finale" from the *William Tell Overture* composed by Gioachino Rossini. We activated the experience with a parachute! The instructional focus included Steady Beat and Form. Share a musical moment with your child by listening to this exciting piece of music together.

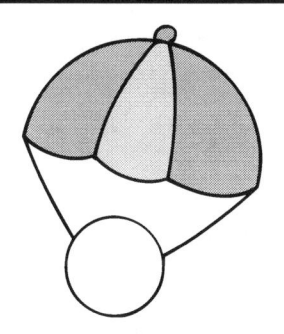

FAMILY MUSICAL MOMENT

Today in music class we listened to the "Finale" from the *William Tell Overture* composed by Gioachino Rossini. We activated the experience with a parachute! The instructional focus included Steady Beat and Form. Share a musical moment with your child by listening to this exciting piece of music together.

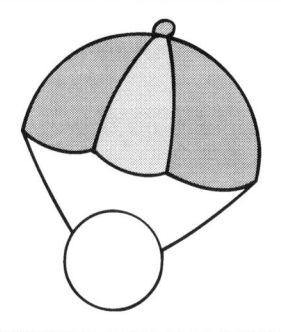

FAMILY MUSICAL MOMENT

Today in music class we listened to the "Finale" from the *William Tell Overture* composed by Gioachino Rossini. We activated the experience with a parachute! The instructional focus included Steady Beat and Form. Share a musical moment with your child by listening to this exciting piece of music together.

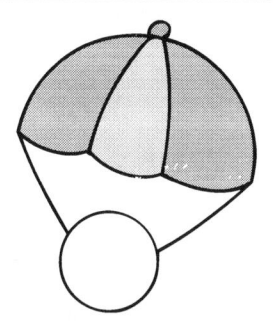

FAMILY MUSICAL MOMENT

Today in music class we listened to the "Finale" from the *William Tell Overture* composed by Gioachino Rossini. We activated the experience with a parachute! The instructional focus included Steady Beat and Form. Share a musical moment with your child by listening to this exciting piece of music together.

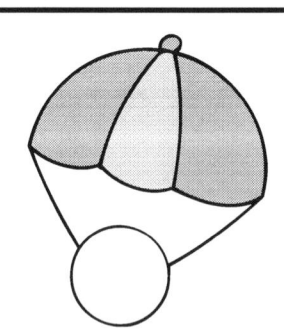

FAMILY MUSICAL MOMENT

Today in music class we listened to the "Finale" from the *William Tell Overture* composed by Gioachino Rossini. We activated the experience with a parachute! The instructional focus included Steady Beat and Form. Share a musical moment with your child by listening to this exciting piece of music together.

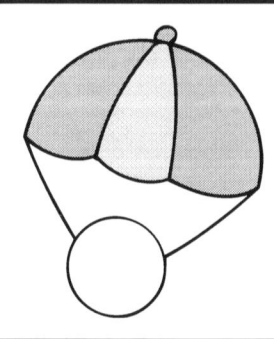

Suggested Grade Levels: 3–5

Flashlight Activity

"Finale" to the Overture from *William Tell*

By Gioachino Rossini (1792–1868)

Your children are going to rave about this unique listening lesson! My students ask to "flashlight paint" again and again. They even have friends bring flashlights to sleepovers so they can recreate the activity at home.

Materials

Recording—Track 1
Form Chart (see page 10)
A flashlight for each student
Black bulletin-board paper

Preparation

Use black bulletin-board paper to cover your classroom windows for this activity. It is well worth the trouble as the darker the room, the more powerful the musical experience! At Bear Lake I cover my windows with sheets of black bulletin-board paper by taping it to the wall above the window. (My plan room is stocked with rolls and rolls of this paper.) When not in use, I roll up the sheet and secure it with a paper clip on each side (think roller blind). Then, when you're ready to flashlight paint, unroll the paper and you're ready to go. I do the same with the window in my door, being sure to roll the paper back up the moment the lesson is over, due to fire department regulations.

You'll need a lot of flashlights for this activity. I put a request for flashlights in our school newsletter and received more than enough. Other cost-saving tips:

1. Be sure to take out the batteries if you will not be using the flashlights in the near future. The batteries last longer this way and you don't have to worry about batteries corroding in (and ruining) your flashlights.

2. In the fall of each year, I put batteries on the Music Wish List that runs in the school newsletter. Again, my parents come through in spades.

In order to represent the sections of this piece, a third of the flashlights need red lenses, a third need green lenses, and a third need purple (or blue) lenses. (You'll also need a flashlight with a clear lens for yourself!) While you can buy colored lighting gels, I simply colored the clear lenses with permanent markers.* I'm not sure why but I've never had any luck using blue permanent markers to color the lenses, so I stick with red, green, and purple. For easy distribution during the lesson, store the flashlights in baskets, with each color in its own basket.

Before teaching this lesson, you'll want to practice this piece a number of times to feel comfortable with the complex form. Cueing accurate entrances and section changes is of great importance to the success of the activity. When you're ready to present this in your classroom, start by discussing the form of the piece along with the non-pitched percussion and parachute play activities, if you taught either of these in previous lessons or years.

---
* A shout-out to my friend Erin McRary for this idea. What an easy, quick solution!

PARACHUTES AND RIBBONS AND SCARVES, OH, MY!

INSTRUCTIONAL STEPS

1. Share or review the folk legend of William Tell.

2. Display the Form Chart for this piece (found on page 10) and discuss it with the children. Music vocabulary words to address include:

    a. Introduction

    b. Interlude

    c. Coda

    d. Steady Beat

3. Explain to the students that they will be listening to a famous piece of music and interpreting that piece of music through a painting activity. The canvas, however, will be the classroom ceiling (or a wall, if your ceiling doesn't work) and the paintbrushes will be flashlights. Students will need to listen carefully to their assigned section and paint patterns on the ceiling with their flashlights that match the beat, tempo, dynamics, and mood of their section. (Many of my students comment how this is similar to laser light shows they've seen.) If this is the students' initial experience with the *Finale to the Overture to William Tell*, it would be advisable to listen to the piece once before distributing the flashlights.

4. Assign each student to one of three groups:

    - Red-Lens Flashlights = A Section
    - Green-Lens Flashlights = B Section
    - Purple-Lens Flashlights = C Section

    Let the children know that you will "paint" during the Introduction, Interludes, and D Section, and that all flashlights will paint during the Coda. Position the groups so that they are all facing forward and can see you. Do not distribute the flashlights yet.

5. Establish and discuss behavior guidelines for the activity. It is critical to the musical integrity of the piece that the children do not turn their lights on or off, or play with their lights when it is not their assigned time to paint. Explain to them that this dishonors the very music that is the basis of the lesson. Tell them that, with no exceptions, children who are not following directions and who are using their flashlights improperly will have the flashlight taken from them. Inform the students that they will have practice time once the flashlights have been distributed and the lights have been turned off.

    Emphasize the fact that no talking is allowed during guided-listening activities, even very exciting ones like this. (My students get very excited and noisy when the flashlights are first distributed, and it takes a little while to lead them back into listen-to-directions mode.) **Give all directions before distributing flashlights,** and then give the children time to experiment with them. Tell the students that they won't see the true impact of the flashlights on the ceiling until you turn off the lights. Remind them that the reason we are using the flashlights today is to interpret and demonstrate what we hear in the music.

"Finale" to the Overture from William Tell

6. Instruct the students to lie down on the floor to paint. They love this! I stand front and center and ask them all to lay on the floor with their feet toward me, which helps with the line-of-sight. Once they are in position, I use student helpers to distribute the flashlights. Turn off the lights and allow the children to practice painting patterns on the ceiling directly above their heads. They may also practice painting circles and *Beat Stripes* that cover the entire ceiling.

7. Review the Form Chart and brushstrokes. *Beat Stripes* are created by moving the flashlight in a straight path to the beat of the music. As the name suggests, *Wild Wiggles* are quick, wiggly patterns made with short, quick, irregular, side-to-side movement of the light. *Half-Note Curves* are comma-like shapes, made to the half-note pulse. All painting happens above the students' heads and should match the theme being heard.

8. Perform the routine, calling cues throughout the piece. Be sure to speak your cues as one section is ending so that students may start the next section on time. Tell the students to have their thumbs on the On/Off switch at all times, so that they can quickly turn off the flashlight if it's on during the wrong section.

    Introduction: You paint with a clear flashlight during the famous trumpet call.

    A Section: Students with the red lenses paint patterns.

    B Section: Students with the green lenses paint patterns. Ask students to really show the powerful beat of this section with large, strong painting motions.

    Interlude: You paint.

    A Section: Students with the red lenses paint.

    C Section: Students with the purple lenses paint. This section begins with a strong beat that can be shown and is followed by very fast rhythmic patterns in the strings.

    D Section: You paint during this section. I like to show the rhythm of the string bass part, then change to the fast-and-furious violin part. I go back to painting the bass part before the section ends.

    C Section: Students with the purple lenses paint.

    B Section: Students with the green lenses paint with large, strong motions.

    Interlude: You paint.

    A Section: Students with the red lenses paint again.

    Coda: All students paint during this section. The routine follows, but it's a long coda, so feel free to improvise with motions of your own. Before you start reading the following routine, I suggest cueing up the Coda so you can listen to it while going through the directions. They make sense with the music, I promise!

    - *Beat Stripes*, all going the same direction, for 6 measures. (24 beats)
    - Meet in one of the front corners for *Wild Wiggles* for 4 beats, change to the other corner for 4 beats, then back to first corner for 4 beats, and finally change to second corner again for 4 beats. (16 beats)
    - Large circles for 2 measures. (8 beats)
    - *Beat Stripes* for 6 measures. (24 beats)
    - Repeat *Wild Wiggles* section. (16 beats)

Parachutes and Ribbons and Scarves, Oh, My!

- Large circles for 2 measures. (8 beats)
- Turn off the flashlights after the long descending melody. On the whole note, come back in with 4 beats of *Wild Wiggles*.
- *Beat Stripes* for 2 measures. (8 beats)
- Eight large *Half-Note Curves*. (16 beats)

Turn off the flashlights and keep them off until the final note. On the final note, all painters do *Wild Wiggles* all over the ceiling, going to complete dark on the cut-off.

You'll want to practice the Coda a number of times on your own before you teach it to children. It is very musically intense and will be the most passionate part of the lesson. The students will leave your room begging for more, and will want to download the piece as soon as they get home.

9. Give your students a Family Musical Moment note as they leave so they can find the music online.

Activity at a Glance

Introduction	Teacher
A Section	Red
B Section	Green
Interlude	Teacher
A Section	Red
C Section	Purple
D Section	Teacher
C Section	Purple
B Section	Green
Interlude	Teacher
A Section	Red
Coda	See directions on pages 16–17

Family Musical Moment

Today in music class we listened to the "Finale" from the *William Tell Overture* composed by Gioachino Rossini. We activated the experience with flashlight painting. The instructional focus included Steady Beat and Form. Share a musical moment with your child by listening to this exciting piece of music together.

Family Musical Moment

Today in music class we listened to the "Finale" from the *William Tell Overture* composed by Gioachino Rossini. We activated the experience with flashlight painting. The instructional focus included Steady Beat and Form. Share a musical moment with your child by listening to this exciting piece of music together.

Family Musical Moment

Today in music class we listened to the "Finale" from the *William Tell Overture* composed by Gioachino Rossini. We activated the experience with flashlight painting. The instructional focus included Steady Beat and Form. Share a musical moment with your child by listening to this exciting piece of music together.

Suggested Grade Levels: K–5

Moving with Scarves

The Syncopated Clock

By Leroy Anderson (1908–1975)

All my Bear Lake students love this catchy piece of music. This lesson will definitely be the most joyful part of your teaching day!

Materials

Recordings—Tracks 2 and 3
27" scarves (one for every student)
Vocabulary Flash Cards* (see pages 22–25)

Instructional Steps

1. Ask the students to describe the vocabulary terms *staccato*, *legato*, triangle, and coda. You might use the questions below, placing the corresponding flashcard on the board after each correct answer.

   "Raise your hand if you can tell me the musical term for short, separated notes." (*Staccato*)
   "What is the opposite of staccato—long, smooth, connected notes?" (*Legato*)
   "What is the name of percussion instrument whose name is the same as its shape?" (Triangle)
   "What is the word for the ending section of a composition?" (Coda)

2. Describe rondo form, and consider drawing an iconic representation on the board. I usually draw the following pattern on the board:

   ○ □ ○ △ ○

   Ask the students to label the form with the correct alphabet letters. Then, ask the children if anyone remembers the name of a musical form in which the A Section keeps returning, separated by contrasting sections. I will often use the simple description, "A—something new—A—something new—A." When the correct answer is determined, write the term *Rondo* on the board.

3. Distribute the scarves to the students who are seated around the room. Be sure to remind them to find their own personal space and not sit too close to other students. Lead the children in preparatory movements for each section as described below:

   A Section: Walk to the steady beat throughout the room, showing short, *staccato* motions with the scarf. Remind students to use all of their levels: high, middle, and low.

---

* All of the visuals in this book are also available online. See page 6 for more details.

B Section: Remain in one place and hold the scarf in both hands. Sway back and forth to the beat, holding the scarf in front of you. At the end of each four-measure segment, do a full turn, swinging the scarf—still held in both hands—above your head.

C Section: Place the scarf into the hand with which you write. Wiggle it quickly down low and then toss it into the air on each roll of the triangle, using the same hand to both toss and catch the scarf. There will be two tosses, then two more measures of music in which you will turn in a circle while waving the scarf in horizontal wiggles (sort of snaky in shape). In my classroom, we call these turn/wiggles "Twirly Whirlies." This sequence of two tosses and a *Twirly Whirlie* will repeat four times during the C Section.

Activity at a Glance	
A Section	Staccato walk
B Section	Sway and turn
A Section	Staccato walk
C Section	Tosses and *Twirly Whirlies*
A Section	Staccato walk
Coda	Toss and catch

Coda: Hold the scarf in two hands and toss it into the air just before the last note of the piece. Catch it somewhere on your body, using *no hands* for the catch. I tell the children that they can catch it on their head, shoulders, arms, foot, bootie—wherever—as long as it's not caught with their hands!

4. Perform the piece. Be sure to remind your students that there is no talking allowed during guided-listening activities. Be ready, however, for lots of smiles as children perform this upbeat routine. My kindergartners usually can't contain the hoots of joy as they toss the scarves during the C Section of the music.

5. Finish the lesson with a beautiful piece of scarf-folding music. I use Leroy Anderson's *Forgotten Dream*, although any music of a peaceful nature will work. As the giggles subside from the scarves landing on their heads at the end of the rondo routine, ask the children to lay their scarves flat on the floor. As the music begins to play, I call the following directions:

   Use two hands and fold your square scarf into a rectangle.
   Use two hands and fold the rectangle into a square.
   Use two hands and fold the square into a rectangle.
   Use two hands and fold the rectangle into a square.
   Thank you for bringing your scarf forward and placing it neatly into the scarf basket!

6. Give your students a Family Musical Moment note (found on page 26) as they leave so they can find the music online.

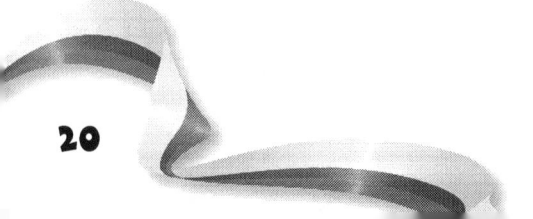

Form Chart: The Syncopated Clock

A A B A C CODA

The original purchaser of *Parachutes and Ribbons and Scarves, Oh My!* (30/2626H) by Artie Almeida has permission to reproduce this page for use in his or her classroom setting. © 2011 Heritage Music Press, a division of The Lorenz Corporation.

Staccato

Legato

The original purchaser of *Parachutes and Ribbons and Scarves, Oh My!* (30/2626H) by Artie Almeida has permission to reproduce this page for use in his or her classroom setting. © 2011 Heritage Music Press, a division of The Lorenz Corporation.

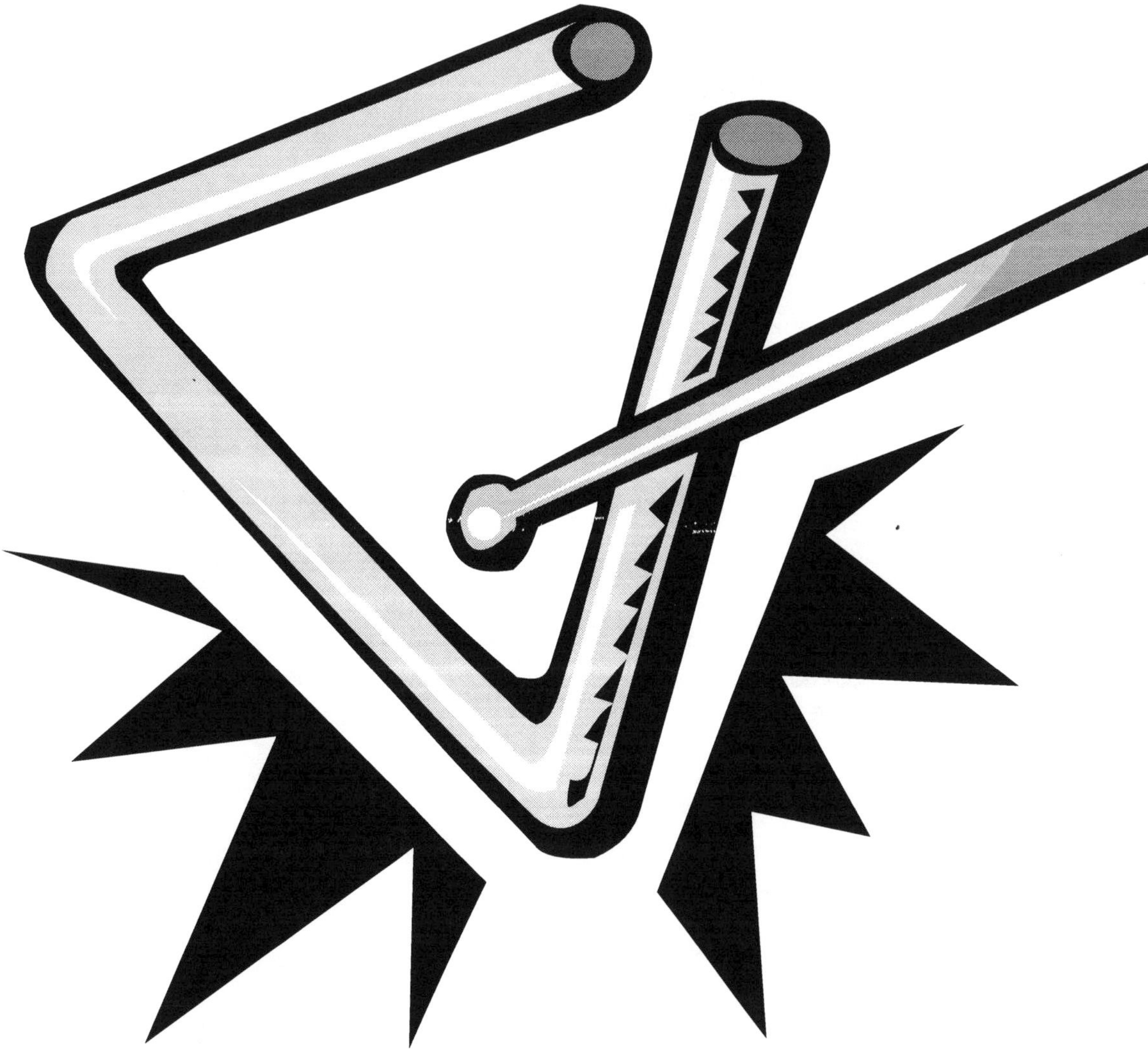

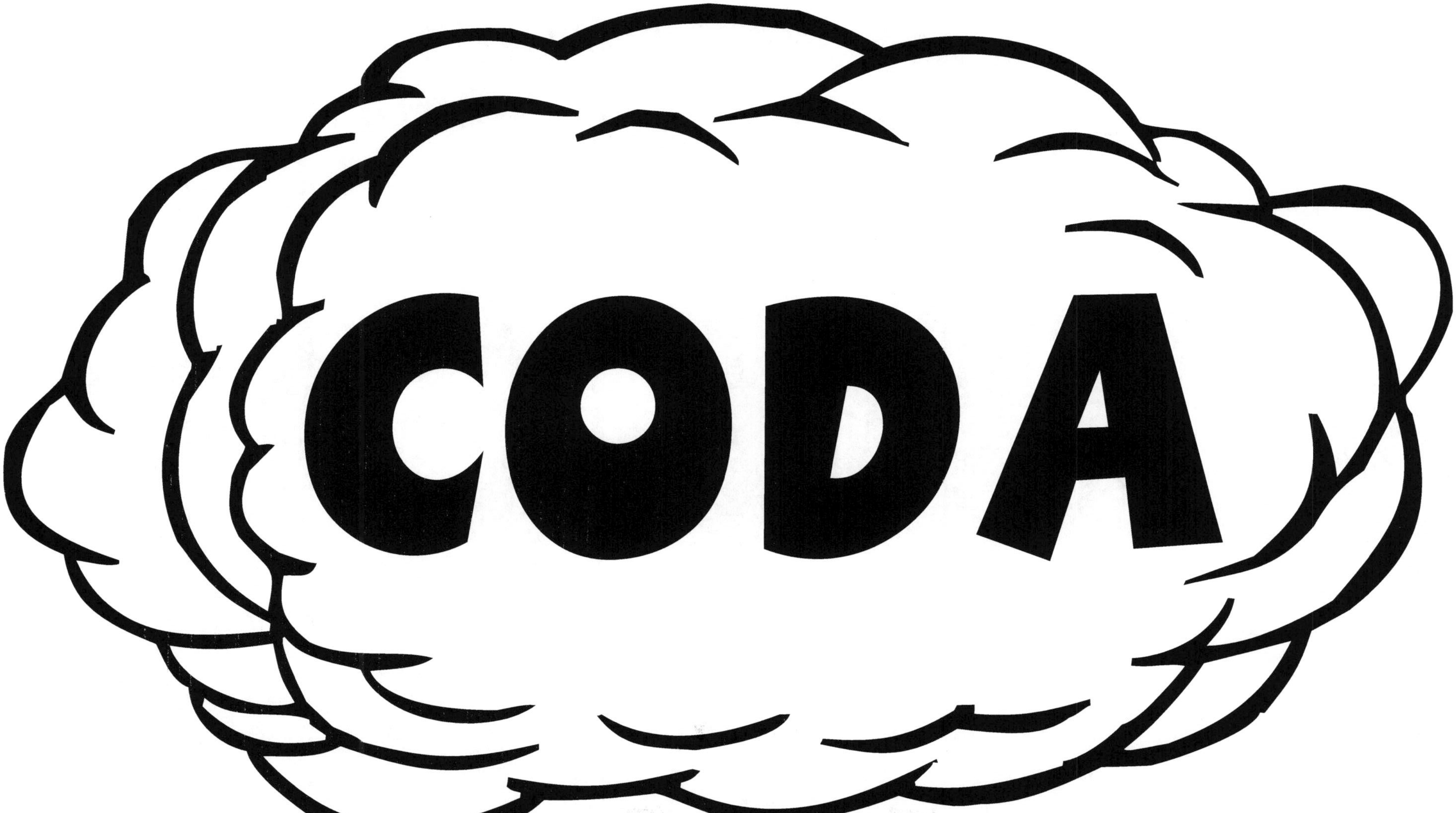

The original purchaser of *Parachutes and Ribbons and Scarves, Oh My!* (30/2626H) by Artie Almeida has permission to reproduce this page for use in his or her classroom setting. © 2011 Heritage Music Press, a division of The Lorenz Corporation.

PARACHUTES AND RIBBONS AND SCARVES, OH, MY!

FAMILY MUSICAL MOMENT

Today in music class we listened to *The Syncopated Clock* composed by Leroy Anderson. We activated the experience with scarves. The instructional focus included Steady Beat, Rondo Form, and the musical terms *Staccato*, *Legato*, and *Coda*. Share a musical moment with your child by listening to this exciting piece of music together.

FAMILY MUSICAL MOMENT

Today in music class we listened to *The Syncopated Clock* composed by Leroy Anderson. We activated the experience with scarves. The instructional focus included Steady Beat, Rondo Form, and the musical terms *Staccato*, *Legato*, and *Coda*. Share a musical moment with your child by listening to this exciting piece of music together.

FAMILY MUSICAL MOMENT

Today in music class we listened to *The Syncopated Clock* composed by Leroy Anderson. We activated the experience with scarves. The instructional focus included Steady Beat, Rondo Form, and the musical terms *Staccato*, *Legato*, and *Coda*. Share a musical moment with your child by listening to this exciting piece of music together.

FAMILY MUSICAL MOMENT

Today in music class we listened to *The Syncopated Clock* composed by Leroy Anderson. We activated the experience with scarves. The instructional focus included Steady Beat, Rondo Form, and the musical terms *Staccato*, *Legato*, and *Coda*. Share a musical moment with your child by listening to this exciting piece of music together.

FAMILY MUSICAL MOMENT

Today in music class we listened to *The Syncopated Clock* composed by Leroy Anderson. We activated the experience with scarves. The instructional focus included Steady Beat, Rondo Form, and the musical terms *Staccato*, *Legato*, and *Coda*. Share a musical moment with your child by listening to this exciting piece of music together.

Suggested Grade Levels: K–3

Giddy-up! A Stick-Horse Adventure

The Wild Horseman

By Robert Schumann (1810–1856)

Begin with puppets and then saddle up and ride!

Materials
Recording—Track 4
Form Chart (see page 29)
2 Horse Finger Puppets
Stick Horses*

Instructional Steps

1. Tell the children the title and composer of the piece.

2. Display your two horse puppets and ask the children to name them. Solicit name suggestions and choose two that are appealing to the children. Ask the children to greet each horsey by name.

3. Discuss the AABA form, while placing the Form Chart on the board or projecting it electronically. Explain to the children that the first horse gets to gallop on the A Sections and the second horse will gallop on the B Section. (In the video demo, the first horse is named Midnight; the second is Caramel.) Ask your students which horse gets to have the most fun. (Answer: Midnight—because he gets to gallop a lot.)

4. Invite the children to use their hands as horses while you demonstrate the form activity with your puppets. Start the music and gallop one horse during the A Sections and the other horse during the B Section. Repeat the entire activity with the other horse galloping on the A Sections. Be sure to call out "The A Section repeats!" on the second A, as some children won't catch this melody feature.

5. Position your students in their "barn" locations. I instruct all the boys to line up on one side of the room in their "row of horse stalls" and all the girls to line up in their barn on the opposite side of the room, facing the boys.

6. Distribute stick horses, a few at a time. Consider calling children to get a horse by the month in which they were born, hair color, pets owned, etc. Just for fun we "groom" the stick horses, give them some snacks out of our pockets, choose a name for them, and give them a drink of water before we ride.

7. For the first experience, assign one team to ride on the A Sections. The other team will ride during B. Tell them that you will be helping them hear the section changes by calling cues. (I always give a little heads up when each section is nearing its end.) Start the music and enjoy the children's squeals of joy as they ride to this exciting piece!

---
* It's best if your horse puppets are two different colors. The Mary Meyer Trotters Horse Tippy Toes finger puppets, which are what I use, are available in several colors. Get the stick horses from a dollar store.

PARACHUTES AND RIBBONS AND SCARVES, OH, MY!

8. For the second experience, change jobs—the team that rode on the A Sections now rides on B, and vice versa.

9. As a final experience, instruct all students to ride their horses (at a gallop) around the meadow (empty space in the room) during the A Sections and let their horses graze (by freezing in place) during the B Section. By the end of the final A Section, all students should be home in the barn. Be sure to give a verbal cue to help all the horses make it home by the last note.

10. Give your students a Family Musical Moment note as they leave so they can find the music online.

FAMILY MUSICAL MOMENT

Today in music class we listened to *The Wild Horseman* composed by Robert Schumann. We activated the experience with stick horses. The instructional focus included Steady Beat and AABA Form. Share a musical moment with your child by listening to this exciting piece of music together.

FAMILY MUSICAL MOMENT

Today in music class we listened to *The Wild Horseman* composed by Robert Schumann. We activated the experience with stick horses. The instructional focus included Steady Beat and AABA Form. Share a musical moment with your child by listening to this exciting piece of music together.

FAMILY MUSICAL MOMENT

Today in music class we listened to *The Wild Horseman* composed by Robert Schumann. We activated the experience with stick horses. The instructional focus included Steady Beat and AABA Form. Share a musical moment with your child by listening to this exciting piece of music together.

FAMILY MUSICAL MOMENT

Today in music class we listened to *The Wild Horseman* composed by Robert Schumann. We activated the experience with stick horses. The instructional focus included Steady Beat and AABA Form. Share a musical moment with your child by listening to this exciting piece of music together.

Form Chart: The Wild Horseman

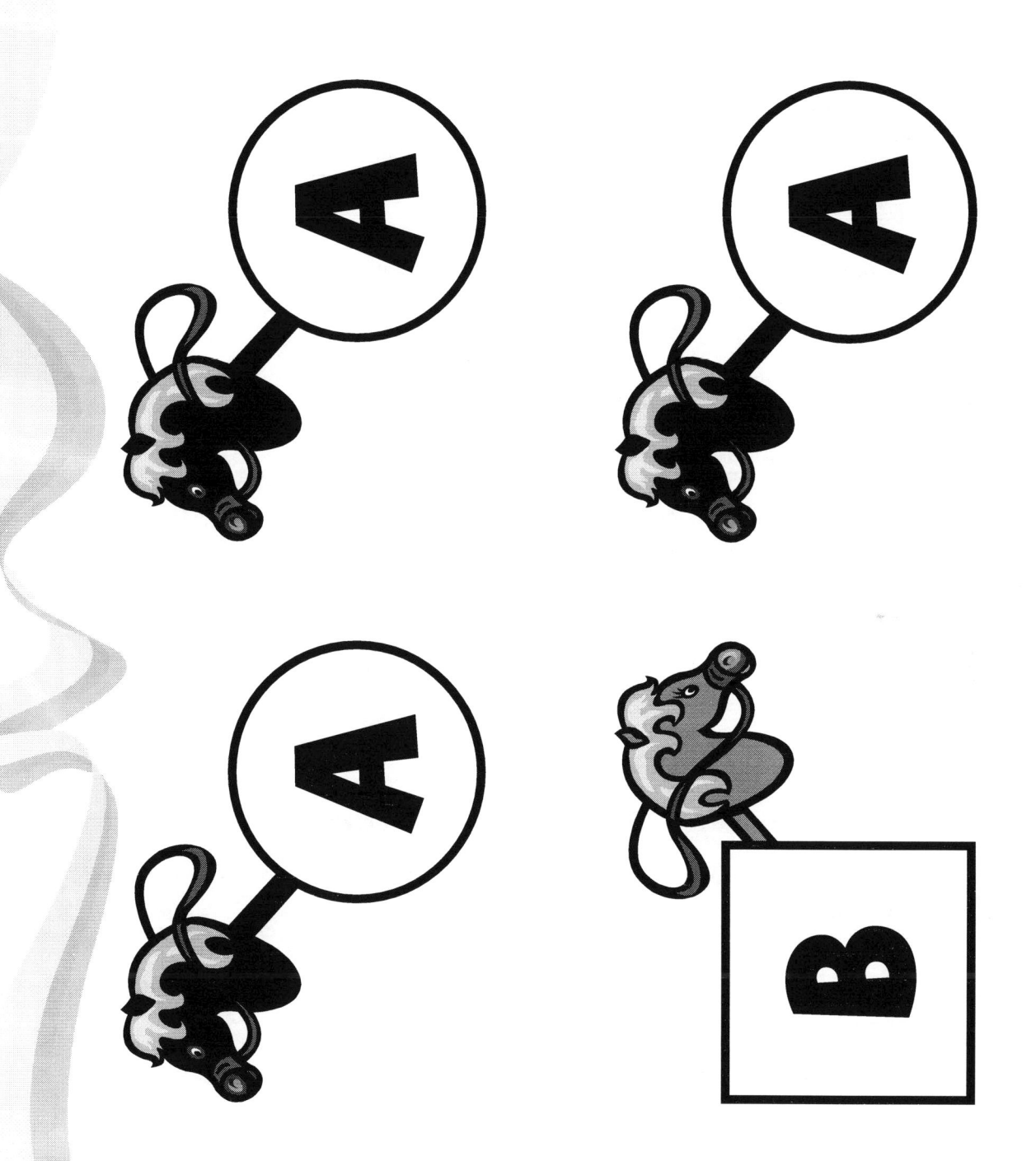

A A

A B

The original purchaser of *Parachutes and Ribbons and Scarves, Oh My!* (30/2626H) by Artie Almeida has permission to reproduce this page for use in his or her classroom setting. © 2011 Heritage Music Press, a division of The Lorenz Corporation.

A Ribbon Streamer Movement Activity

"Galop" from *The Comedians*

By Dimitri Kabalevsky (1904–1987)

Suggested Grade Levels: K–5

Your students will enjoy this exhilarating piece of music and the ribbon-streamer activity that illuminates the form and melodic direction.

MATERIALS

Recording—Track 5
Ribbon Streamers*
Form Chart (see page 32)

INSTRUCTIONAL STEPS

1. Write *Composer* on the board and call on a student to define the term.

2. Share the following five fun facts about the composer of "Galop":

   - He was born in St. Petersburg, Russia.
   - His birthday is December 30, 1904. How old would he be if he were alive today?
   - His main instrument had 88 keys. What was it?
   - He also loved to paint and write poetry.
   - Many composers only write music, but Dimitri was very interested in music education and loved teaching young children.

3. Explain that today's featured listening piece was written by Dimitri Kabalevsky in 1938. Share with students that, because its general form is ABA, they will hear two main melodies. The first melody will be followed by a contrasting melody, and then the first melody will return. The more detailed form of this piece is:

   Introduction   A   Interlude   A   Interlude   B   Interlude   A   Interlude   A

   A—Interlude—A serves as one, larger A Section, which returns at the end after a longer interlude that borrows much of its musical material from the Introduction.

   Let your students know that the music in the A Section will repeat, but that the introduction will not. Explain that an interlude is a short section of music between two larger sections; it is like a bridge to get from one large section to the next.

4. Ask the students to predict what the tempo and mood of this piece might be, based on its title.

5. For the first experience, listen to the piece while leading the children in hand motions that will prepare them for the streamer activity. (See the ribbon patterns listed on the next page, or simply watch the video before you read the rest of this lesson plan.) During the B Section, pantomime playing the xylophone, then the violin.

   When finished listening to the piece, discuss the melodic motive of the A Section and how it matched the "Zorro-type" motions (the musical line descends and the Zs move from high to low). Also ask the stu-

---

* For K–2 students, I use 3' streamers. I use 7' streamers for with older elementary students.

"Galop" from The Comedians

dents what instruments they think were mimed during the B Section (xylophone and violin).

6. If you desire, use the Form Chart for visual assistance while teaching this lesson. Using a ribbon streamer, demonstrate the components of the ribbon dance. Allow the students to practice each movement before starting the music and performing the routine.

Introduction: Point the streamer downward and do quick circles, making a spiral pattern. Turn around one revolution, while maintaining spirals, and snap the ribbon to a stop on the ground on the last note of the introduction. This movement pattern, which we call "Fire," will be used in the Introduction as well as during the Interlude that leads back into the second A—Interlude—A, which has the same music as the Introduction.

A Sections: Start with the ribbon high and make Zs back and forth (a Zorro-type pattern) toward the ground on the first two measures of the A Section. This matches the descending line of music. Now, swing the ribbon up high and to the right side, then up high and to the left side. Finish the A Section with a full circle from low to high and back, in front of the body. Do this pattern twice.

Interludes: Wave the ribbon back and forth in front of you on the floor. It should look like a snake is slithering back and forth from your left to your right, or vice versa. This will be used for the Interludes between the A repetitions (within the large A Section) and for the Interlude approaching the B Section. We refer to this movement as "Snakes in the Grass." Please note that during the first interlude after the B Section, I perform *Fire* rather than *Snakes in the Grass* because the music matches the Introduction and serves the same musical function, which is to prepare us for the A Section.

B Section: Pantomime playing the xylophone and violin in appropriate places.

Final Chord: Raise both hands in a "V" above your head.

7. Give your students a Family Musical Moment note (found on page 33) as they leave so they can find the music online.

Activity at a Glance

Introduction	*Fire*
A Section	Zorro, swings, and circle (repeat)
Interlude	*Snakes in the Grass*
A Section	Zorro, swings, and circle (repeat)
Interlude	*Snakes in the Grass*
B Section	Miming instruments
Interlude	*Fire* (Introduction music returns)
A Section	Zorro, swings, and circle (repeat)
Interlude	*Snakes in the Grass*
A Section	Zorro, swings, and circle (repeat)
	Hands up on the final chord!

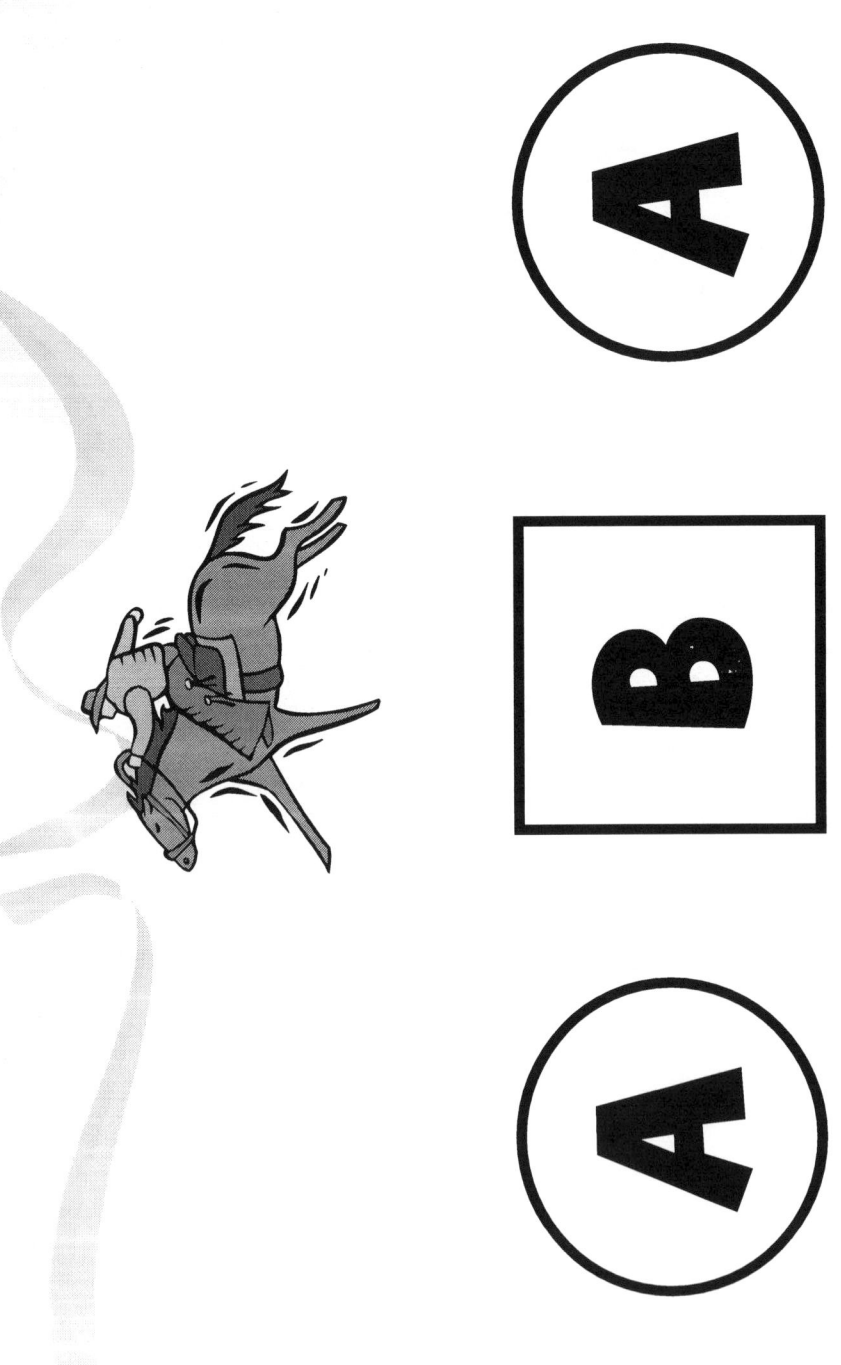

Form Chart: "Galop" from *The Comedians*

A

B

A

"Galop" from The Comedians

Family Musical Moment
Today in music class we listened to a piece called "Galop" from *The Comedians* composed by Dimitri Kabalevsky. Our instructional focus included Melodic Direction and ABA Form. We activated the lesson with ribbon streamers. Share a musical moment with your child by listening to this exciting piece of music together.

Family Musical Moment
Today in music class we listened to a piece called "Galop" from *The Comedians* composed by Dimitri Kabalevsky. Our instructional focus included Melodic Direction and ABA Form. We activated the lesson with ribbon streamers. Share a musical moment with your child by listening to this exciting piece of music together.

Family Musical Moment
Today in music class we listened to a piece called "Galop" from *The Comedians* composed by Dimitri Kabalevsky. Our instructional focus included Melodic Direction and ABA Form. We activated the lesson with ribbon streamers. Share a musical moment with your child by listening to this exciting piece of music together.

Family Musical Moment
Today in music class we listened to a piece called "Galop" from *The Comedians* composed by Dimitri Kabalevsky. Our instructional focus included Melodic Direction and ABA Form. We activated the lesson with ribbon streamers. Share a musical moment with your child by listening to this exciting piece of music together.

Family Musical Moment
Today in music class we listened to a piece called "Galop" from *The Comedians* composed by Dimitri Kabalevsky. Our instructional focus included Melodic Direction and ABA Form. We activated the lesson with ribbon streamers. Share a musical moment with your child by listening to this exciting piece of music together.

A Form Lesson Activated with Plastic Plates

"March" from *The Nutcracker*
By Pyotr Ilyich Tchaikovsky (1840–1893)

Suggested Grade Levels: K–5

> **The Nutcracker:** *It's not just for Christmas anymore! I use the pieces from this wonderful ballet throughout the year. They are fabulous for teaching form, and the children always recognize the melodies. My little ones will often shout, "I've heard that music! I love that music!" So, don't feel limited to using these pieces just in the month of December.*
>
> *This activity began its life as a classroom lesson on rondo form. It then became an ensemble performance piece due to student demand. The children loved this activity and their parents just ate it up at the concert. Most of the families had never heard of guided-listening lessons, so it was a wonderful opportunity to share with them how these types of activities are an important part of my curriculum to focus on music analysis.*

Materials
Recording—Track 6
Plastic plates, two per student with a few extra in case of breakage*
Form Chart (see page 37; optional)

Instructional Steps
1. Display a visual of the form of the March. Consider first using shapes (see below) and then labeling each of the shapes with a letter name (ABACABA), or you can use the Form Chart found on page 34.

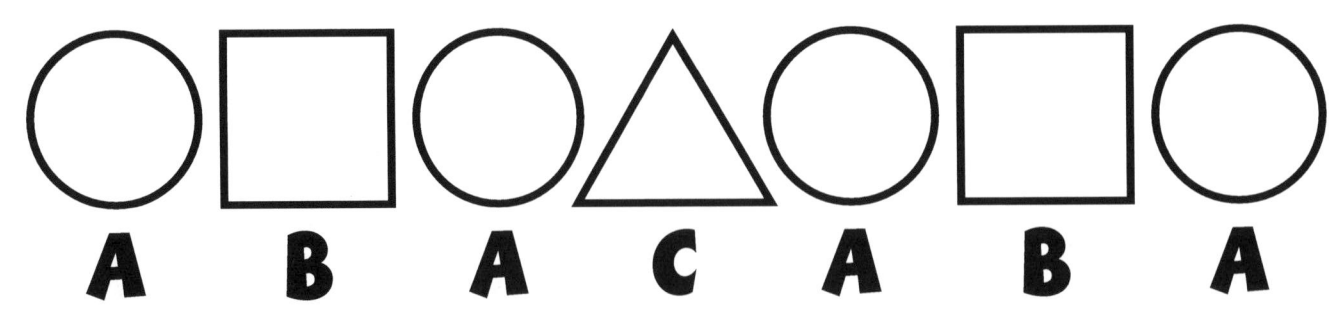

A B A C A B A

---

* I use eight-inch plastic plates. Paper plates are a possibility, but I prefer the durability and percussive sound of the plastic. The eight-inch size looks the best on stage, although if you are working with very young children, you might consider the six-inch size. Red, green, and white plates make for a festive presentation during the holidays. If you are doing this at a time of year other than the holidays, just pick any three colors of plates you wish.

"March" from The Nutcracker

2. Listen to the piece once through, helping the students to discover the rondo form. Note that the A Section has two distinct parts: one which has a marching feel, followed by a section that sounds like galloping music. Those two parts then repeat, making the A Section rather long.

3. To prepare for the use of the plates, listen to the recording again and lead your students to perform the following hand motions on their laps for each section, pretending they are holding plates: Pat laps, clap plates together, hold plate out to sides by face, clap plates together.

4. Arrange the children on risers (or seated in the classroom chairs or on the floor) and divide them into three groups. Distribute red plates (or any other color of your choosing) to the group on the left, white plates to the group in the middle, and green plates to the group on the right. Have the children hold their plates with their thumbs against the back of the plate and their fingers extending over the rim and resting on the flat bottom of the plate. To begin, all students should hold their plates in a starting position. We use "mouse ears"—holding the plates against our heads and above our ears, so we look like Mickey Mouse.

A Section: *All plates*
Listen to the first two measures of the A Section to hear the beat. Move the plates to the music following this pattern: Pat laps, clap plates together, hold out to sides by face, clap plates together. Repeat this sequence four times. Then, wave the plates from right to left to a half-note beat. Change the waving to a quarter-note beat to match the music. This works out to be four half-note waves and seven quarter-note waves. Repeat the entire sequence.

B Section: *Red plates only*
Pat the bottom of plates together, alternating with the right plate on top, then the left, like patting out a tortilla, eight times. We call these "taco claps." Next, pat alternating eighth notes on laps. Repeat both parts.

A Section: *All plates*
All plates repeat the A Section.

C Section: *White plate only*
Wave the plates upward in a wiggly motion for four beats, then back down in the same fashion. We call this "flying dots." Next, have the students fan themselves with the plates while leaning to their right for four beats, then to their left for four beats. Repeat both parts.

A Section: *All plates*
All plates repeat the A Section.

Second B Section: *Green plates only*
Brush the bottoms of the plates together in large, sweeping motions for eight beats. Then, do an eight-beat drum roll on laps with the plates.

Final A Section: *All plates*
Pat laps, clap plates together, hold out above heads in a "V," clap plates together. Repeat this sequence four times. Then, wave the plates from right to left to a half-note beat. Change the waving to a quarter-note beat to match the music. (As before, this works out to be four half-note waves and seven quarter-note waves.)

PARACHUTES AND RIBBONS AND SCARVES, OH, MY!

Repeat the entire sequence, but on the last section of the half-note and quarter-note waves, change the last four beats of the piece to: clap, clap, clap, up. The plates should be raised up above the head (arms in a "V") to freeze on the final note. We like to put both plates together and "tip our hats" to the audience at the end.

5. Give your students a Family Musical Moment note as they leave so they can find the music online.

> **ACTIVITY AT A GLANCE**
>
> | | |
> |---|---|
> | A Section | All plates |
> | B Section | Red plates only |
> | A Section | All plates |
> | C Section | White plates only |
> | A Section | All plates |
> | B Section | Green plates only |
> | A Section | All plates |

FAMILY MUSICAL MOMENT

Today in music class we listened to the "March" from the ballet *The Nutcracker* composed by Pyotr Ilyich Tchaikovsky. Our instructional focus included Rondo Form and Steady Beat. We activated the lesson with plastic plates. Share a musical moment with your child by listening to this exciting piece of music together.

FAMILY MUSICAL MOMENT

Today in music class we listened to the "March" from the ballet *The Nutcracker* composed by Pyotr Ilyich Tchaikovsky. Our instructional focus included Rondo Form and Steady Beat. We activated the lesson with plastic plates. Share a musical moment with your child by listening to this exciting piece of music together.

FAMILY MUSICAL MOMENT

Today in music class we listened to the "March" from the ballet *The Nutcracker* composed by Pyotr Ilyich Tchaikovsky. Our instructional focus included Rondo Form and Steady Beat. We activated the lesson with plastic plates. Share a musical moment with your child by listening to this exciting piece of music together.

Form Chart: "March" from *The Nutcracker*

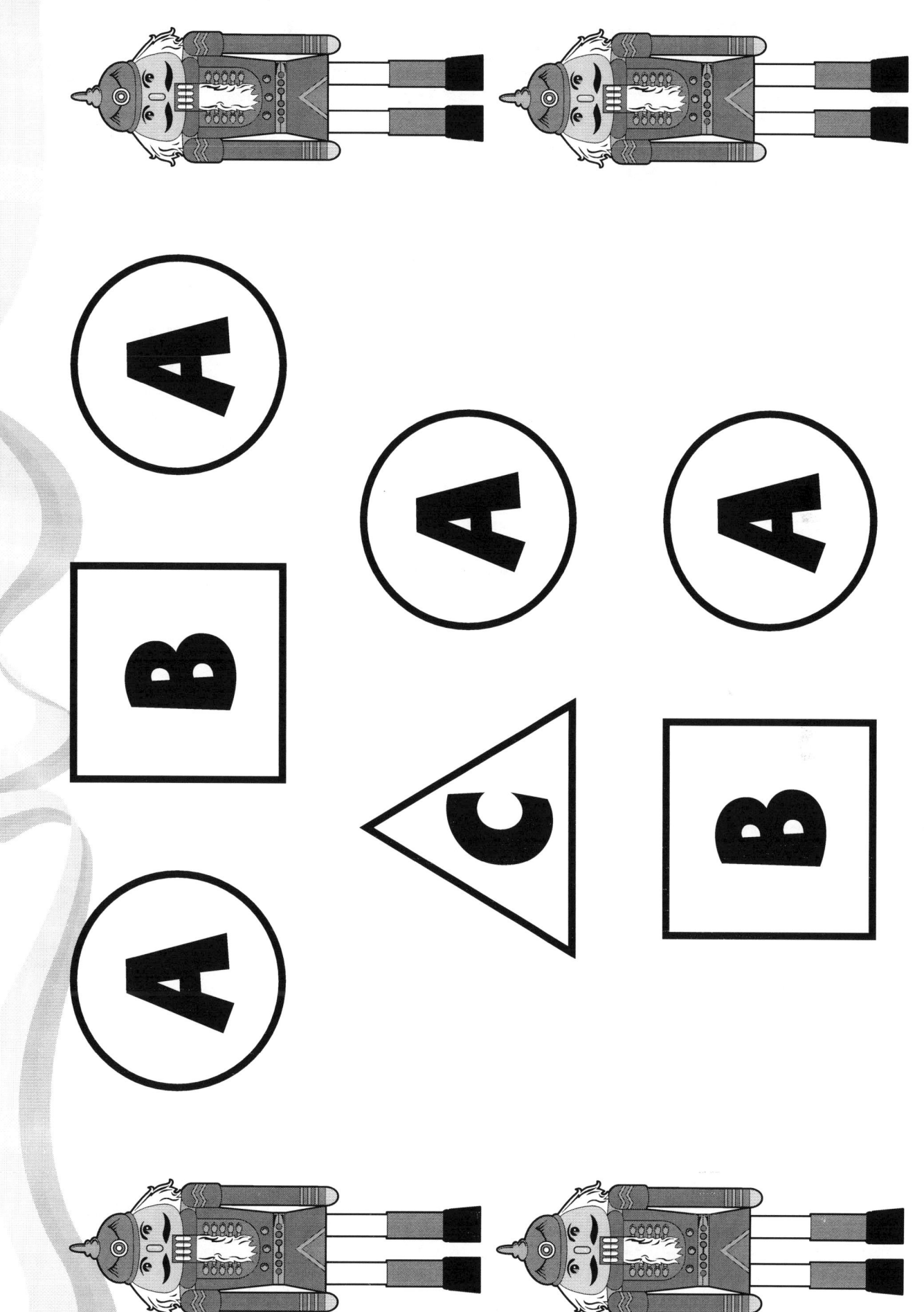

A B A
   A
   C B
   A

The original purchaser of *Parachutes and Ribbons and Scarves, Oh My!* (30/2626H) by Artie Almeida has permission to reproduce this page for use in his or her classroom setting. © 2011 Heritage Music Press, a division of The Lorenz Corporation.

A Form Lesson Activated with Large Plastic Candy Canes

"March" from *The Nutcracker*
By Pyotr Ilyich Tchaikovsky (1840–1893)

Suggested Grade Levels: K–3

> A number of years ago one of my neighbors was having a garage sale in December. They had a bucket of large candy-cane yard decorations. I figured I would buy them and use them to decorate my classroom. The next day my kindergartners were getting ready to ride their stick horses to the "March" from *The Nutcracker* when I decided it would be hilarious to have them ride these new candy-cane horses! They hooted and hollered and it made for the cutest picture. So now those candy canes come out every December. I think your children will also appreciate the humor in this! Tie a red holiday ribbon around the "horses'" necks for a more festive look.

Materials
Recording—Track 6
Large plastic candy-cane yard decorations (enough for half of your class)
Jingle bells and egg shakers (enough for the other half of your class)

Instructional Steps

1. Display a visual of the form of the "March." Consider first using shapes (see below) and then labeling each of the shapes with a letter name (ABACABA).

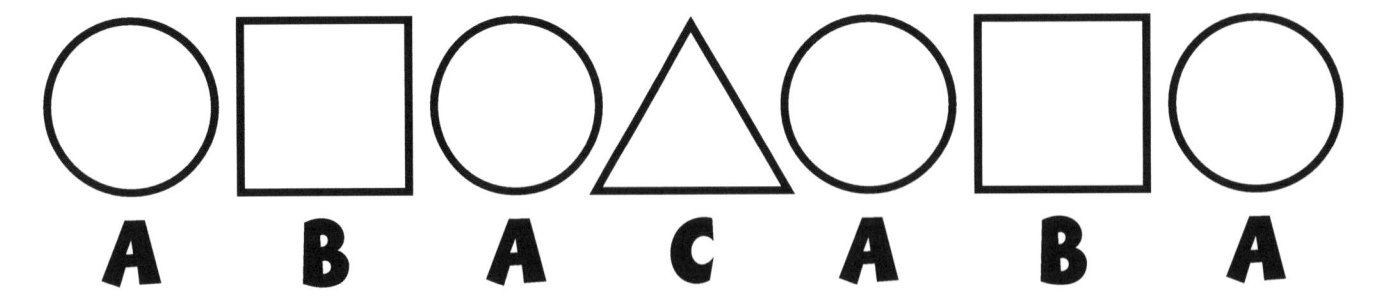

A B A C A B A

2. Listen to the piece once through, helping the students to discover the rondo form. Note that the A Section has two distinct parts, one which has a marching feel, followed by a section that sounds like galloping music. Then, those two parts repeat, making the A Section rather long.

"March" from The Nutcracker

3. Divide the class into two groups. One half will ride the candy-cane horses, while the other half plays jingle bells and egg shakers on the A Sections. Repeat the activity, switching groups, so that all of the children get to experience both parts. If you wish, allow the children to name their horses and then "groom" them.

Activity at a Glance	
A Section	Horses march and gallop to the music
B Section	Horses graze
A Section	Horses march and gallop to the music
C Section	Feed the horses treats
A Section	Horses march and gallop to the music
B Section	Horses drink from the lake
A Section	Horses march and gallop to the music

A Section: Listen to the first two measures of the A Section to hear the beat. Have half of the children march and gallop during the A Section. The music clearly dictates the movement. Remember that both parts repeat, so they march/gallop/march/gallop for each A Section. This is clearly heard in the music. The other half of the children sit in a row to the side, playing the steady beat on the jingle bells while the horses march, and shaking the egg shakers (or maracas) quickly while the horses gallop.

B Section: Children face the center and tip their horse's head down to "graze."

Repeat the A Section

C Section: Children face the center and "feed" their horses treats from their pockets. Carrots, celery, apples, oats, etc.—no sugar cubes, please!

Repeat the A Section

Second B Section: Children face the center and let their horse "drink from the lake."

Repeat the A Section

At the end of the piece, have the children groom their horses and thank them for the ride.

4. Give your students a Family Musical Moment note (found on page 40) as they leave so they can find the music online.

PARACHUTES AND RIBBONS AND SCARVES, OH, MY!

FAMILY MUSICAL MOMENT
Today in music class we listened to the "March" from the ballet *The Nutcracker* composed by Pyotr Ilyich Tchaikovsky. Our instructional focus included Rondo Form and Steady Beat. We activated the lesson with Large Plastic Candy Canes. Share a musical moment with your child by listening to this exciting piece of music together.

FAMILY MUSICAL MOMENT
Today in music class we listened to the "March" from the ballet *The Nutcracker* composed by Pyotr Ilyich Tchaikovsky. Our instructional focus included Rondo Form and Steady Beat. We activated the lesson with Large Plastic Candy Canes. Share a musical moment with your child by listening to this exciting piece of music together.

FAMILY MUSICAL MOMENT
Today in music class we listened to the "March" from the ballet *The Nutcracker* composed by Pyotr Ilyich Tchaikovsky. Our instructional focus included Rondo Form and Steady Beat. We activated the lesson with Large Plastic Candy Canes. Share a musical moment with your child by listening to this exciting piece of music together.

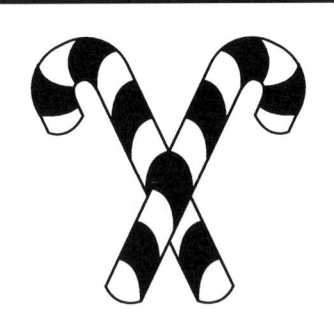

FAMILY MUSICAL MOMENT
Today in music class we listened to the "March" from the ballet *The Nutcracker* composed by Pyotr Ilyich Tchaikovsky. Our instructional focus included Rondo Form and Steady Beat. We activated the lesson with Large Plastic Candy Canes. Share a musical moment with your child by listening to this exciting piece of music together.

FAMILY MUSICAL MOMENT
Today in music class we listened to the "March" from the ballet *The Nutcracker* composed by Pyotr Ilyich Tchaikovsky. Our instructional focus included Rondo Form and Steady Beat. We activated the lesson with Large Plastic Candy Canes. Share a musical moment with your child by listening to this exciting piece of music together.

Suggested Grade Levels: 2–5

A Form Lesson Activated with a Stretchy Band

"March" from *The Nutcracker*

By Pyotr Ilyich Tchaikovsky (1840–1893)

Use a stretchy band to reinforce the rondo form of this favorite! My students love using our stretchy band. They've named him "Super Stretchy" and cheer whenever he comes out of the storage closet.

Materials

Recording—Track 6
Stretchy band*
1 sheet each of red, blue, green, orange, yellow, and purple colored paper (or the colors that match the sections of your stretchy band)

Instructional Steps

1. Display a visual of the form of "March" from *The Nutcracker*. Consider first using shapes (see below) and then asking the children to label each of the shapes with a letter name (ABACABA).

   ○ □ ○ △ ○ □ ○

2. Listen to the piece once through, helping the students to discover the rondo form. Note that the A Section has two distinct parts, one which has a marching feel, followed by a section that sounds like galloping music. Then, those two parts repeat making the A Section rather long. To help students focus on the music, lead them in making marching and galloping gestures on their laps in time to the music. Sit quietly while listening to the B and C Sections. See if the children can hear the return of the A melody without your help by challenging them to make the motions when the A Section returns.

3. Show the students the stretchy band, and discuss what colors they see. Display the colored pieces of paper you have that correspond to the colors of your stretchy band. Explain that these cue cards will be used during the B and C Sections.

---

* This activity may also be done with a multi-colored parachute. I find, however, that behavior is better when a stretchy band is used because the students are never out of sight. (In this activity, students will be running under the band, where they can be seen, or under a parachute, where they can't.)

PARACHUTES AND RIBBONS AND SCARVES, OH, MY!

4. Outline the movement activity by sharing the following instructions with your students before starting the music.

   Starting position
   All students will be in a circle, holding the stretchy band with *both hands* on the same color.

   A Section
   When the recording begins, all students will march then gallop, and march then gallop again, matching the music of the A Section. There is no introduction, so the students should listen carefully to start on time. Determine a direction in which to travel.

Activity at a Glance	
A Section	March then Gallop
B Section	Indicated color(s) move
A Section	March then Gallop
C Section	Indicated color(s) move
A Section	March then Gallop
B Section	Indicated color(s) move
A Section	March then Gallop

   B and C Sections
   On each B and C Section, all students will stop galloping, face the center, raise the stretchy band above their heads, and listen for the teacher to call and show a color. Then, the students holding that color will let go of the stretchy band and run under it to find another section that is the same color. (More than one student may be holding each color section.)

   If your stretchy band has six colors, consider calling three colors (one at a time!) during the B and C Sections. For example, you might call red, blue, and green during the B Section, and then orange, yellow, and purple during the C Section.

   When the B Section returns a final time, consider calling two colors at a time, until all six colors have been called. This makes for a very fun, albeit a little frantic, finish to the piece. If your classes are very large, you may choose to call just two colors during the B and C Sections.

5. Give your students a Family Musical Moment note as they leave so they can find the music online.

FAMILY MUSICAL MOMENT

Today in music class we listened to the "March" from the ballet *The Nutcracker* composed by Pyotr Ilyich Tchaikovsky. Our instructional focus included Rondo Form and Steady Beat. We activated the lesson with a giant stretchy band! Share a musical moment with your child by listening to this exciting piece of music together.

FAMILY MUSICAL MOMENT

Today in music class we listened to the "March" from the ballet *The Nutcracker* composed by Pyotr Ilyich Tchaikovsky. Our instructional focus included Rondo Form and Steady Beat. We activated the lesson with a giant stretchy band! Share a musical moment with your child by listening to this exciting piece of music together.

Suggested Grade Levels: K–5

A Form Lesson Activated with Ribbon Wands

"Trepak (Russian Dance)" from *The Nutcracker*

By Pyotr Ilyich Tchaikovsky (1840–1893)

This quick, simple activity is lots of fun for children of all ages!

Materials
Recording—Track 7
3' Ribbon Wands or Strips of silky ribbon
Form Chart (see page 45)

Instructional Steps

1. Display the Form Chart. Ask students to hypothesize what this form might sound like.

2. Survey the class to discover which children have heard of *The Nutcracker* ballet. Explain that the music they are about to hear is the "Russian Dance," or "Trepak," from this famous ballet.

3. Play the recording while leading the class in hand motions that match the routine, while children are seated. See the directions below for motions to imitate.

4. Distribute the ribbon wands, and ask the children to spread out throughout the room.

5. Before starting music, practice each step of the routine outlined below with the streamers.

A Section
Wave the ribbon up and down quickly; repeat.

Turn in place while waving the ribbon (*Turning Flourishes*).

Repeat both moves

Second A Section
Jump and wave the ribbon up and down quickly; repeat.

Turning Flourishes

Repeat

B Section
Wave the ribbon back and forth while pointing it downward for eight beats (*Wash the Floor*).

Wave the ribbon back and forth while pointing it upward for eight beats (*Wash the Windows*).

Repeat.

Parachutes and Ribbons and Scarves, Oh, My!

Interlude

Wave the ribbon up to one side quickly, then to the other.

Repeat the motions again quickly, matching the rhythm of music.

Third A Section

Jump and wave the ribbon up and down quickly; repeat.

Turning Flourishes

Repeat both moves

Coda

Wash the Floor for eight beats, then *Wash the Windows* for eight beats.

Turning Flourishes for six beats

Jump and finish with the ribbons up and arms out above head!

Activity at a Glance

A Section	Up and down then *Turning Flourishes*
A Section	Jump! Up and down then *Turning Flourishes*
B Section	*Wash the Floor* and then *Wash the Windows*
Interlude	Side to side
A Section	Jump! Up and down then *Turning Flourishes*
Coda	*Wash the Floor* (8 beats). *Wash the Windows* (8 beats). *Turning Flourishes* (6 beats). Jump and finish with the ribbons up and arms out above head!

6. Give your students a Family Musical Moment note as they leave so they can find the music online.

Family Musical Moment

Today in music class we listened to "Trepak" from the ballet *The Nutcracker* composed by Pyotr Ilyich Tchaikovsky. Our instructional focus included AABA Form. We activated the lesson with ribbon wands. Share a musical moment with your child by listening to this exciting piece of music together.

Family Musical Moment

Today in music class we listened to "Trepak" from the ballet *The Nutcracker* composed by Pyotr Ilyich Tchaikovsky. Our instructional focus included AABA Form. We activated the lesson with ribbon wands. Share a musical moment with your child by listening to this exciting piece of music together.

Family Musical Moment

Today in music class we listened to "Trepak" from the ballet *The Nutcracker* composed by Pyotr Ilyich Tchaikovsky. Our instructional focus included AABA Form. We activated the lesson with ribbon wands. Share a musical moment with your child by listening to this exciting piece of music together.

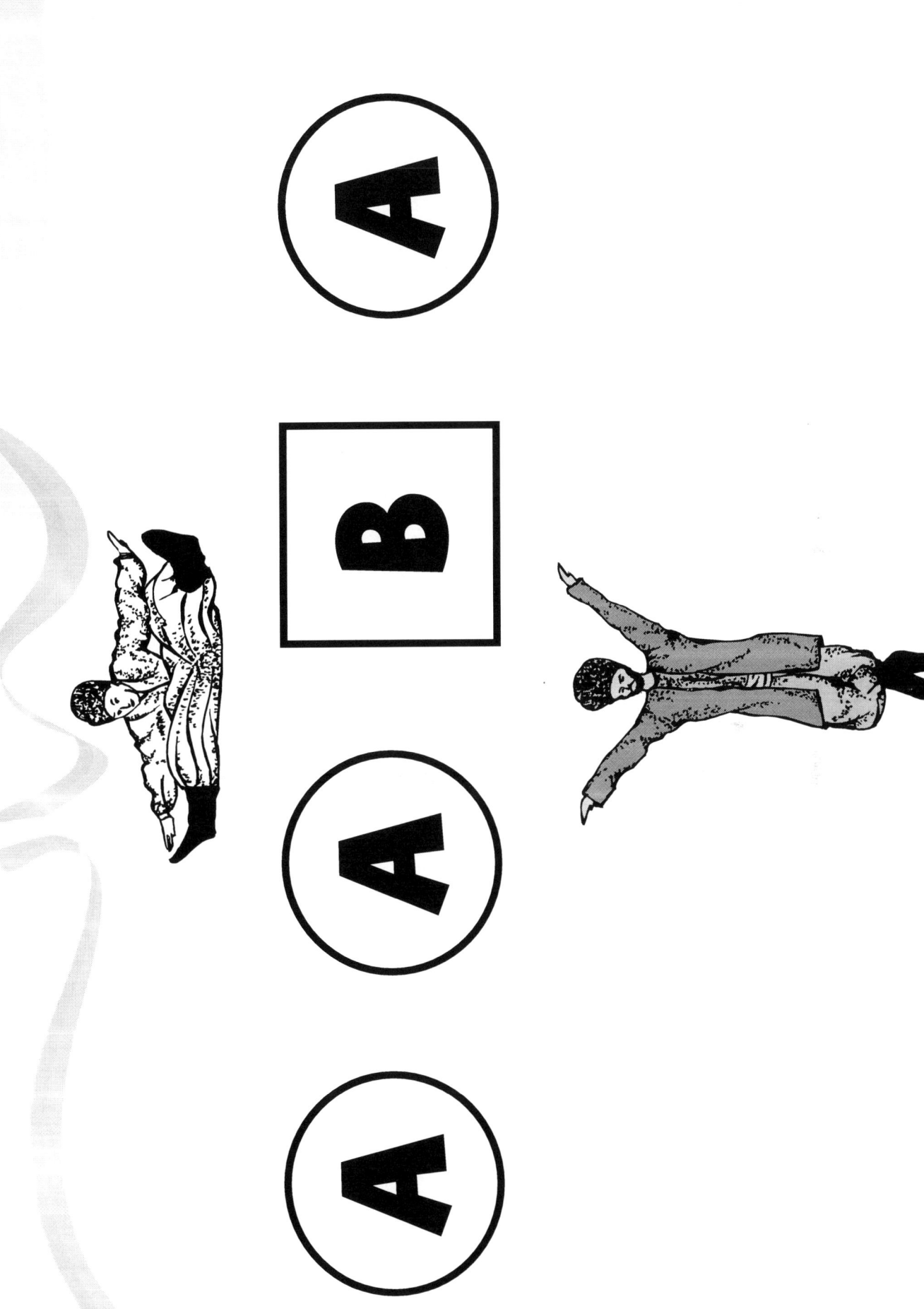

Form Chart: "Trepak (Russian Dance)" from *The Nutcracker*

A A B A

The original purchaser of *Parachutes and Ribbons and Scarves, Oh My!* (30/2626H) by Artie Almeida has permission to reproduce this page for use in his or her classroom setting. © 2011 Heritage Music Press, a division of The Lorenz Corporation.

– 7 –

A Form Lesson Activated with Parachute Play

"Trepak (Russian Dance)" from *The Nutcracker*

By Pyotr Ilyich Tchaikovsky (1840–1893)

Suggested Grade Levels: K–5

Get out the parachute and enjoy the shouts of joy as children experience this exciting piece!

Materials

Recording—Track 7
12' Parachute*
Form Chart (see page 45)

Instructional Steps

1. Display the Form Chart. Discuss.

2. Survey the class to discover which children have heard of the ballet *The Nutcracker*. Explain that the music they are about to hear is the "Russian Dance," or "Trepak," from the famous ballet.

3. To prepare the activity, have the children remain seated and lead them through the parachute-routine hand motions, which are outlined below.

4. Arrange the parachute in the center of the room, and ask the children to make a circle around it.

5. Practice each step of the routine with the parachute before starting the music.

   A Section: Shake the parachute once quickly up and down on each of the two strong beats (whole-note values), then shake the parachute for eight quarter-note beats. Repeat.

   Second A Section: Repeat the A-Section motions, but add jumps on the whole-note-value shakes.

   B Section: Turn to the right and jog in a circle, holding the parachute tightly stretched out. Halfway through the section, turn and jog in the other direction.

   Interlude: Face the center and do two large shakes to whole-note values, then two half-note value shakes, then four quarter-note shakes. This pattern is easily heard in the music.

   A Section: Jump and shake the parachute once quickly up and down on each of the two strong beats (whole-note values), then shake the parachute for eight quarter-note beats (no jumping). Repeat.

---

* I use a twelve-foot parachute for a class of thirty. If you do not own a parachute, you can probably borrow one from your Physical Education department. If you have large classes, and the room to accommodate a bigger parachute, a twenty-foot 'chute is super fun!

46

Trepak (Russian Dance) from The Nutcracker

Coda: Do *The Washing Machine* for sixteen quarter-note beats. (To do *The Washing Machine*, pull the parachute tight and move it from right to left on the steady beat, like the agitator in a washing machine.) Make a cut-off motion to stop the children from doing *The Washing Machine*. Count to three, and then the children *Go Under the Mountain* by raising the parachute above their heads, stepping in and turning around to grab the parachute from the inside. Then, they should quickly squat, pulling the parachute over them. If they trap the air well, the parachute will stay inflated over them like a mountain. This is especially powerful with a twenty-foot parachute. (The 'chute in the video is twelve feet in diameter.)

6. Give your students a Family Musical Moment note as they leave so they can find the music online.

Activity at a Glance

A Section	Shake
A Section	Shake and add jumps
B Section	Jog
Interlude	Face the center and shake to the music
A Section	Shake with jumps
Coda	Do *The Washing Machine* (16 beats). *Go Under the Mountain*.

Family Musical Moment

Today in music class we listened to "Trepak" from the ballet *The Nutcracker* composed by Pyotr Ilyich Tchaikovsky. Our instructional focus included AABA Form. We activated the lesson with a parachute. Share a musical moment with your child by listening to this exciting piece of music together.

Family Musical Moment

Today in music class we listened to "Trepak" from the ballet *The Nutcracker* composed by Pyotr Ilyich Tchaikovsky. Our instructional focus included AABA Form. We activated the lesson with a parachute. Share a musical moment with your child by listening to this exciting piece of music together.

Family Musical Moment

Today in music class we listened to "Trepak" from the ballet *The Nutcracker* composed by Pyotr Ilyich Tchaikovsky. Our instructional focus included AABA Form. We activated the lesson with a parachute. Share a musical moment with your child by listening to this exciting piece of music together.

Movement with Large Scarves

"Viennese Musical Clock" from the *Háry János Suite*

By Zoltán Kodály (1882–1967)

Suggested Grade Levels: 2–5

> These large scarves are a lot of fun for the children because they are big enough to hide under! I used to do this lesson only with the primary-age children, but the big brothers and sisters insisted on having their turns as "bugs in rugs."

Materials

Recording—Track 8
Form Chart (see page 50)
Picture of a mechanical clock
Large Scarves

Instructional Steps

1. Ask your students to describe rondo form to you in words, and to give an example of a rondo using letters.

2. Display the Form Chart.

3. Provide the students with the following background information on the *Viennese Musical Clock* and project an image of a mechanical clock, if possible:

   Zoltán Kodály, a Hungarian composer, wrote a work called the *Háry János Suite*, which has six movements. All six are based on folk tales, supposedly told long ago by a villager named Háry János. The second movement is called *Viennese Musical Clock*, which is about a clock owned by the Austrian Emperor. At noon each day, the doors of the clock would open and a procession of mechanical soldiers would march out and parade around.

4. Explain to the children that they will be listening for the A Sections in this piece and moving to the beat, while shaking a large scarf. On all of the contrasting sections (B, C, and D) they will hide under the large scarf like "bugs in rugs." Tell them that the goal of the lesson is for them to be able to know when to move and when to hide without you calling cues or helping them. (This usually doesn't happen with my primary-aged students until a review lesson occurs.) Encourage children to memorize the theme of the A Section in order to be successful with the listening activity.

5. With the children seated, listen to the piece once through, calling the section letters while the children pretend to shake scarves to the beat of the A Sections. During the Coda, pretend to toss the scarf four times, catching it the last time on the body without using your hands!

Viennese Musical Clock from the Háry János Suite

6. Have your students spread out in the space and distribute large scarves to each child. Perform the following routine:

    A Sections: Step the steady beat throughout the room, shaking the scarves to the beat. Encourage the children to bunch up the large scarves enough so that they will not drag on the floor and trip them.

    B, C, and D Sections: Have the students hide under their scarves like a "bug in the rug"! This, of course, is the children's favorite part. Encourage the children to listen for the A Section to return and see if they can be ready on their own to move on time, rather than relying on the teacher to announce its return.

    Activity at a Glance

A Section	Step and shake to the beat
B Section	Bug in the Rug
A Section	Step and shake to the beat
C Section	Bug in the Rug
A Section	Step and shake to the beat
D Section	Bug in the Rug
A Section	Step and shake to the beat
Coda	Four tosses, "catch with no hands," freeze

    Coda: The students should toss their scarves into the air four times following the accents in the music. On the fourth time, they should catch the scarf somewhere on their body without using their hands, then freeze in this silly pose for a few seconds after the music stops. Encourage the children to glance around the room at all the funny statues that their classmates have made.

In subsequent lessons, encourage the children to focus on some of the timbral and mood details of the piece. Here are some of the things that I've highlighted with my students:

Introduction	Ask the children to name the instrument they hear that makes this piece sound like a clock (the chimes).
A Section	The orchestra plays, with the piccolo being very present in the sound.
B Section	The trumpet and the woodwinds have a nice conversation.
A Section	The oboe is featured.
C Section	The French horn begins the section and clarinet ends it.
A Section	The flute is featured.
D Section	The mood of this section is completely different. ("D is Different!")
A Section	The orchestra plays, with the trumpet predominating.
Coda	Powerful, lots of accents, big finish!

7. Give your students a Family Musical Moment note (found on page 51) as they leave so they can find the music online.

Form Chart: "Viennese Musical Clock" from the *Háry János Suite*

A A B A C D A A CODA

The original purchaser of *Parachutes and Ribbons and Scarves, Oh My!* (30/2626H) by Artie Almeida has permission to reproduce this page for use in his or her classroom setting. © 2011 Heritage Music Press, a division of The Lorenz Corporation.

Viennese Musical Clock from the Háry János Suite

Family Musical Moment

Today in music class we listened to the *Viennese Musical Clock* composed by Zoltán Kodály. Our instructional goals included Rondo Form and Steady Beat. We activated the lesson with large scarves. Share a musical moment with your child by listening to this exciting piece of music together.

Family Musical Moment

Today in music class we listened to the *Viennese Musical Clock* composed by Zoltán Kodály. Our instructional goals included Rondo Form and Steady Beat. We activated the lesson with large scarves. Share a musical moment with your child by listening to this exciting piece of music together.

Family Musical Moment

Today in music class we listened to the *Viennese Musical Clock* composed by Zoltán Kodály. Our instructional goals included Rondo Form and Steady Beat. We activated the lesson with large scarves. Share a musical moment with your child by listening to this exciting piece of music together.

Family Musical Moment

Today in music class we listened to the *Viennese Musical Clock* composed by Zoltán Kodály. Our instructional goals included Rondo Form and Steady Beat. We activated the lesson with large scarves. Share a musical moment with your child by listening to this exciting piece of music together.

Family Musical Moment

Today in music class we listened to the *Viennese Musical Clock* composed by Zoltán Kodály. Our instructional goals included Rondo Form and Steady Beat. We activated the lesson with large scarves. Share a musical moment with your child by listening to this exciting piece of music together.

Creative Movement Groups

"Viennese Musical Clock" from the *Háry János Suite*

By Zoltán Kodály (1882–1967)

Suggested Grade Levels: 2–5

'Ten Hut! Small groups of "soldiers" enjoy creating their own unique locomotor routines for this piece.

Materials
Recording—Track 8
Form Chart (see page 50)

Instructional Steps

1. Ask your students to describe rondo form to you in words, and to give an example of a rondo using letters.

2. Display the Form Chart.*

3. Listen to the piece one time through and call the section letters, while children choose a way to show the steady beat on each A Section. They may pat their laps, snap their fingers, tap their shoulders, etc. Be sure that the body percussion is soft enough to not disturb the music. On the contrasting sections—B, C, and D—instruct the children to do silent, mechanical-type motions with their arms and upper bodies. Have them think of the mechanical soldiers in the Emperor's Viennese Clock and try to simulate those motions.

4. Define and discuss locomotor and non-locomotor movement: locomotor takes you somewhere, while non-locomotor motions are done in one place.

5. Explain that today everyone will be working in teams of three to create some unique and exciting locomotor routines to move throughout the room on each A Section of this rondo. Provide the following parameters:

    a. All three students must be doing the same thing, or very close to the same thing.

    b. Your team must look like a unit—a unified group.

    c. Try to be *very* creative so your group does not have the same movement plan as the other groups.

6. Give the children time to brainstorm with their groups to create their movements. Assist where necessary.

---

* At this point in the lesson, you may also choose to present information about the *Viennese Musical Clock*. See the previous lesson for a short historical background and picture if desired.

Viennese Musical Clock from the Háry János Suite

7. Call on each group to share their plan with the class. Encourage the students to revise their movements as necessary. Place each group in a starting position to best control the traffic flow. Assign or instruct each group to decide which of them will move first, second, and third.

8. Outline the activity as follows:

    A Sections: All students/groups move throughout room, using the locomotor motions they created. Be sure to ask them to be careful of each other as they move.

    B Section: One child in each group moves in place as a mechanical soldier while the other two children freeze in place.

    C Section: The second child in each group moves as a mechanical soldier (moving in place), while the other two children freeze in place.

    D Section: The third child in each group takes his/her turn as a mechanical soldier (again, in place), while the other two children freeze in place.

    Coda: Everyone takes four bows, and then salutes.

Activity at a Glance	
A Section	Teams of three soldiers move throughout the room
B Section	"One" moves in place
A Section	Teams move
C Section	"Two" moves in place
A Section	Teams move
D Section	"Three" moves in place
A Section	Teams move
Coda	Bow four times, then salute

9. Remind the children that each time the A Section returns, it will be played by a slightly different combination of instruments. Some of the A Sections will feature the entire orchestra, while other A Sections will highlight instruments such as the flute and oboe. The dynamic level will change as well, so children may need to move more quietly on some of the A Sections in order to hear the music.

10. Perform the movement activity with the music.

11. Give your students a Family Musical Moment note (found on page 54) as they leave so they can find the music online.

Family Musical Moment

Today in music class we listened to the *Viennese Musical Clock* composed by Zoltán Kodály. Our instructional goals included Rondo Form. We activated the lesson by creating movement routines with our classmates. Share a musical moment with your child by listening to this exciting piece of music together.

Family Musical Moment

Today in music class we listened to the *Viennese Musical Clock* composed by Zoltán Kodály. Our instructional goals included Rondo Form. We activated the lesson by creating movement routines with our classmates. Share a musical moment with your child by listening to this exciting piece of music together.

Family Musical Moment

Today in music class we listened to the *Viennese Musical Clock* composed by Zoltán Kodály. Our instructional goals included Rondo Form. We activated the lesson by creating movement routines with our classmates. Share a musical moment with your child by listening to this exciting piece of music together.

Family Musical Moment

Today in music class we listened to the *Viennese Musical Clock* composed by Zoltán Kodály. Our instructional goals included Rondo Form. We activated the lesson by creating movement routines with our classmates. Share a musical moment with your child by listening to this exciting piece of music together.

Family Musical Moment

Today in music class we listened to the *Viennese Musical Clock* composed by Zoltán Kodály. Our instructional goals included Rondo Form. We activated the lesson by creating movement routines with our classmates. Share a musical moment with your child by listening to this exciting piece of music together.

Suggested Grade Level: K–3

Guided Listening with Student Responder Packs

Rondo Alla Turca

By Wolfgang Amadeus Mozart (1756–1791)

Activate this fascinating piece with animal responders that correspond to the moods of the music.

Materials

Recording—Track 9
Mozart Scramble Info Sheet
Student Responders
Popsicle sticks
Zip-top bags
Form Chart
    (see page 57)

Preparation

Animal Responders: In order to make this piece appealing to children, I decided to pick a critter to represent each section of the music. The A-Section melody snakes upward, thus the snake. The B Section is very vigorous and marked by a strong steady beat, like a galloping horse. The C Section is *very* busy, reminding me of a bee. The Coda has numerous fluttery passages, like the fluttering of a bird's wings.

Every student in your class will need one of each responder. To make these, copy or print the animal responder pieces on colored cardstock, using a different color of paper for each animal. (Templates are provided on pages 59–62 and there are four responders on each page.) Laminate the pages, and then cut out the individual animal pieces. Tape each piece onto a popsicle stick and place one of each animal into a zip-top bag. Make a class set, with enough packages for your largest class.

Form Chart: Laminate the poster for durability. I attach magnets and display the poster on my magnetic board. You might also display the PDF file, available online, with a projection system or electronic whiteboard.

Info Sheet: Prepare the Mozart Scramble Info Sheet, found on page 58, as a poster, overhead transparency, or project it via your computer.

Instructional Steps

1. Write "SRPOCMEO" on the board and call on a student to unscramble this word. You may give them the clue, "This word is a musical career." (Composer). Ask your students to share the names of any composers they know. Tell them that today's featured piece is called *Ronda Alla Turca* and it was composed by Wolfgang Amadeus Mozart.

2. Display the Mozart Scramble Info Sheet and lead the trivia activity by guiding the students through each statement and the words that must be unscrambled.

3. Display the Form Chart (see page 57). Lead your students in predicting the mood or tempo of each section according to the animal representing it. Remember that the form is ABCBAB/Coda.

PARACHUTES AND RIBBONS AND SCARVES, OH, MY!

4. Distribute the responder packs to the students. Have them check their package to make sure they have four pieces: A/Snake, B/Horse, C/Bee, and Coda/Bird.

ACTIVITY AT A GLANCE	
A Section	Snakes
B Section	Horses
C Section	Bees
B Section	Horses
A Section	Snakes
B Section	Horses
Coda	Birds

5. Discuss the term *virtuoso*, asking your students to predict what it means. Explain that a virtuoso is a person who exhibits outstanding talent of the highest degree and that a *virtuosic* work is a piece of music (or art) that is of superior quality.

6. Explain to the children that they will be watching you while moving their animal responders to each section of the music, illustrating the beat, rhythm, or melodic direction of the section. Let the students know that they will need to look up frequently at the poster to see where they are in the piece. Remind them that "Good musicians always look ahead, and listen ahead." Remind the students that all guided listening is done in silence.

7. Start the recording and lead the students through the motions with their responders as follows:

    A Section (Snakes): Starting low in front of you, snake or weave the responder upwards for two measures, matching the piano music, and then move the snake back and forth (left to right) to the beat for two measures. Repeat. (8 measures)

    Tap the snake on the palm of your hand for four measures. (4 measures)

    Snake the responder upwards for two measures. Move the snake back and forth to the beat for two measures. (4 measures)

    Tap the snake on the palm of your hand for four measures. (4 measures)

    Snake the responder upwards for two measures. Move the snake back and forth to the beat for two measures. (4 measures)

    B Section (Horses): "Gallop" the horse responders back and forth in front of you.

    C Section (Bees): Move the bees to match the contour of the melody throughout this *long* section. As the melody goes on for a length of time, start looking exhausted. Sigh occasionally and prop up your arm (at the elbow) with other hand. This little bit of silliness really illustrates the character of this melody. Busy, busy, busy! As the students begin to wear out, jokingly tell them that their job is easy compared to the workout that the piano player is getting!

    B Section (Horses): Gallop the horse responders back and forth in front of you.

    A Section (Snakes): Repeat as above.

    B Section (Horses): Repeat as above.

    Coda (Birds): Move the bird responders to show the contour of the melody, as well as the rhythmic elements. "Flutter" the responders during the twisting and turning parts. "Fly" the birds to a landing on other hand (I call this "their favorite tree branch") on the last note. Have the birdies take a bow to finish.

8. Give your students a Family Musical Moment note (found on page 63) as they leave so they can find the music online.

Form Chart: Rondo Alla Turca

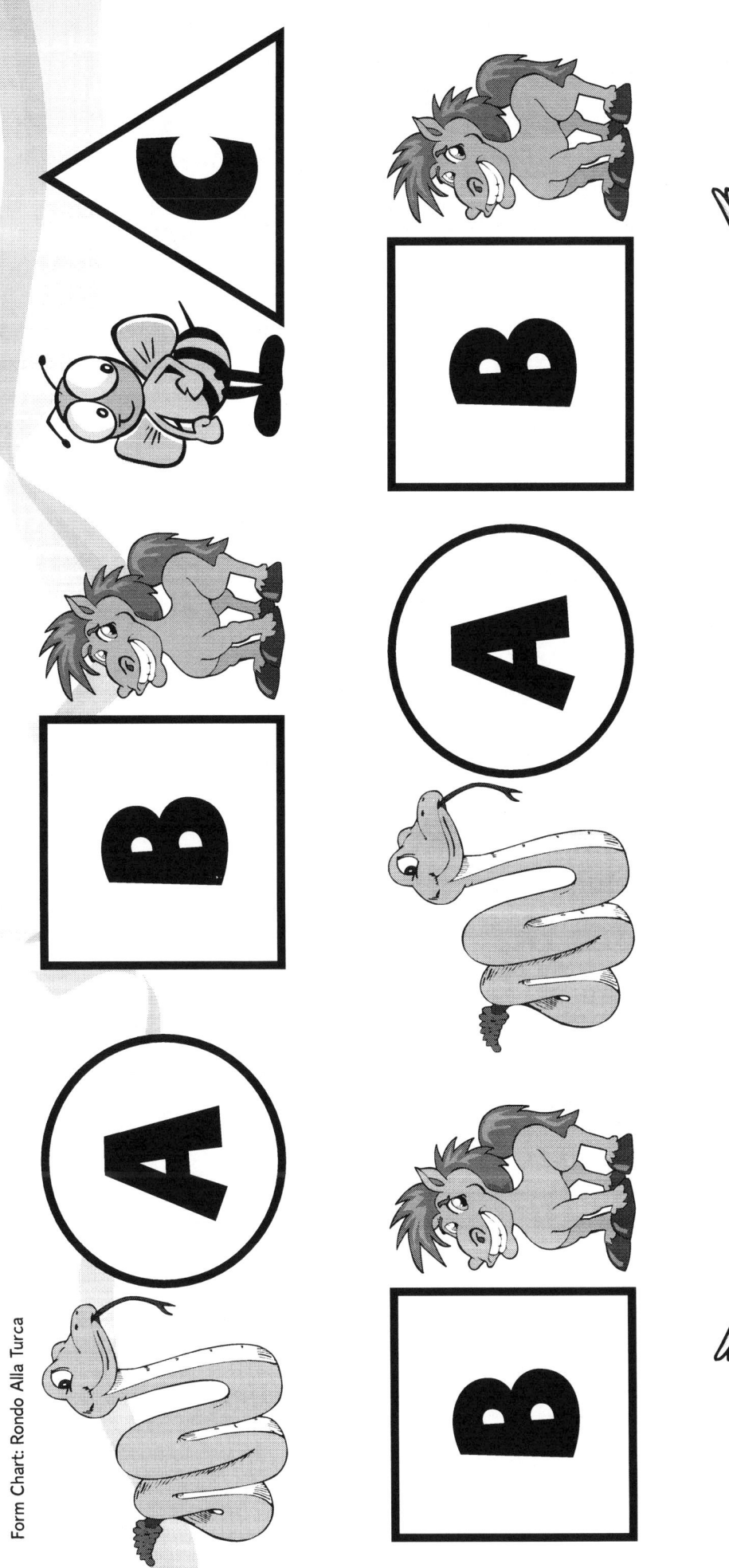

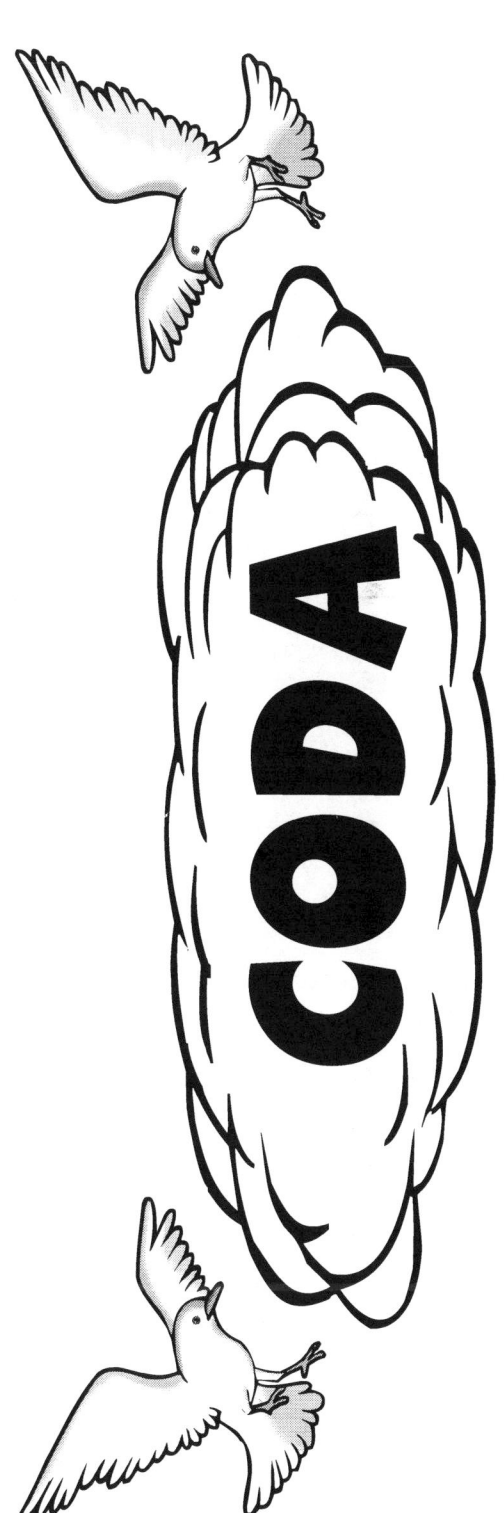

A B A B C B A CODA

Mozart Scramble Info Sheet

1. Mozart's home country was **SAATURI**.

2. Mozart was known as a child **DRGYIPO**, meaning a young person with exceptional abilities.

3. In addition to composing, Mozart played keyboard and **LOINVI**.

4. Mozart composed over **XSI DDUHNER** musical works!

5. His pets included a dog, a horse, and a **NYCAAR**.

Animal Responder Masters

To make your own animal responders, duplicate each of the following pages on cardstock. Then laminate each page and cut out the animal shapes. Mount each shape on a Popsicle stick.

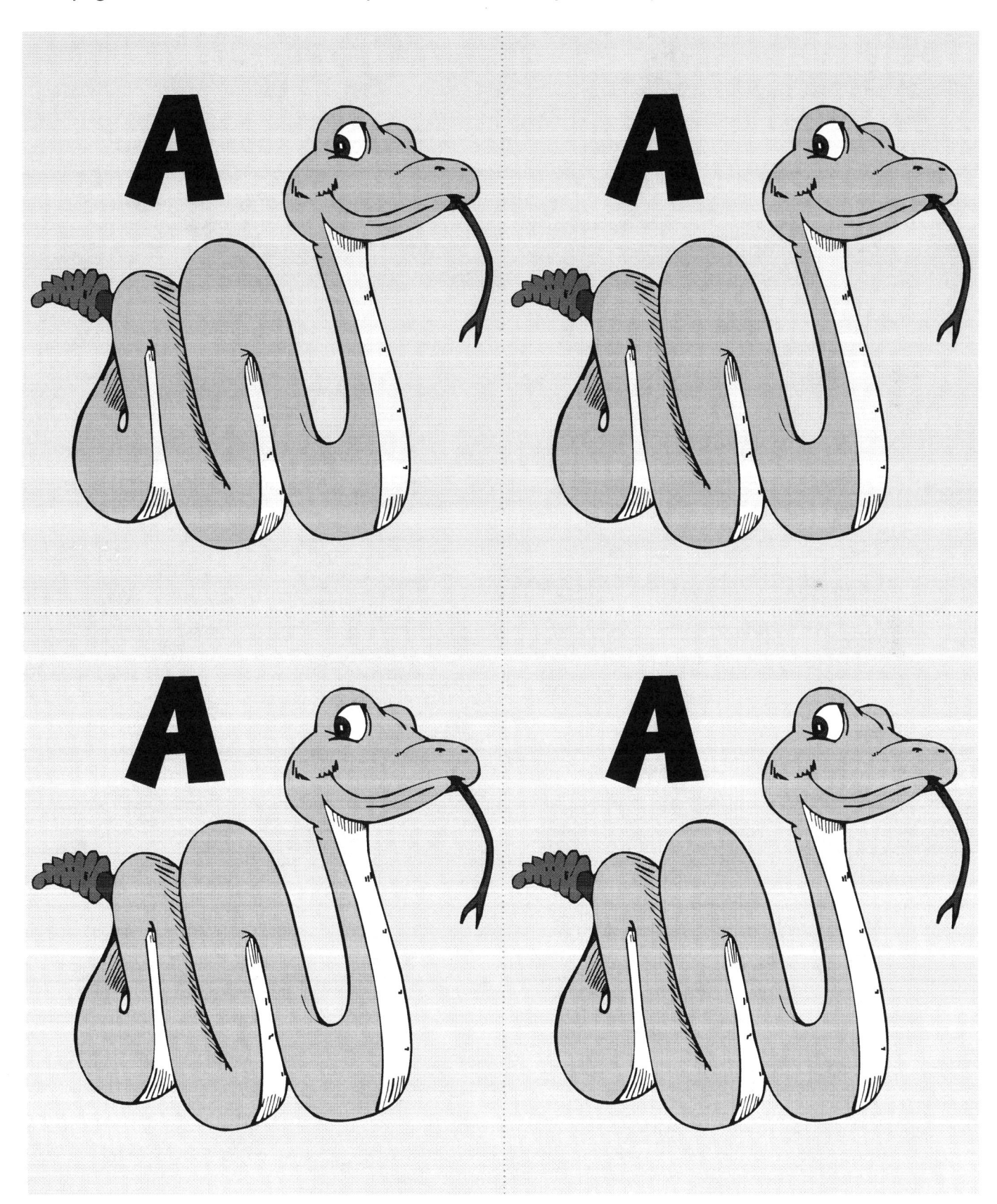

A **A**

A **A**

The original purchaser of *Parachutes and Ribbons and Scarves, Oh My!* (30/2626H) by Artie Almeida has permission to reproduce this page for use in his or her classroom setting. © 2011 Heritage Music Press, a division of The Lorenz Corporation.

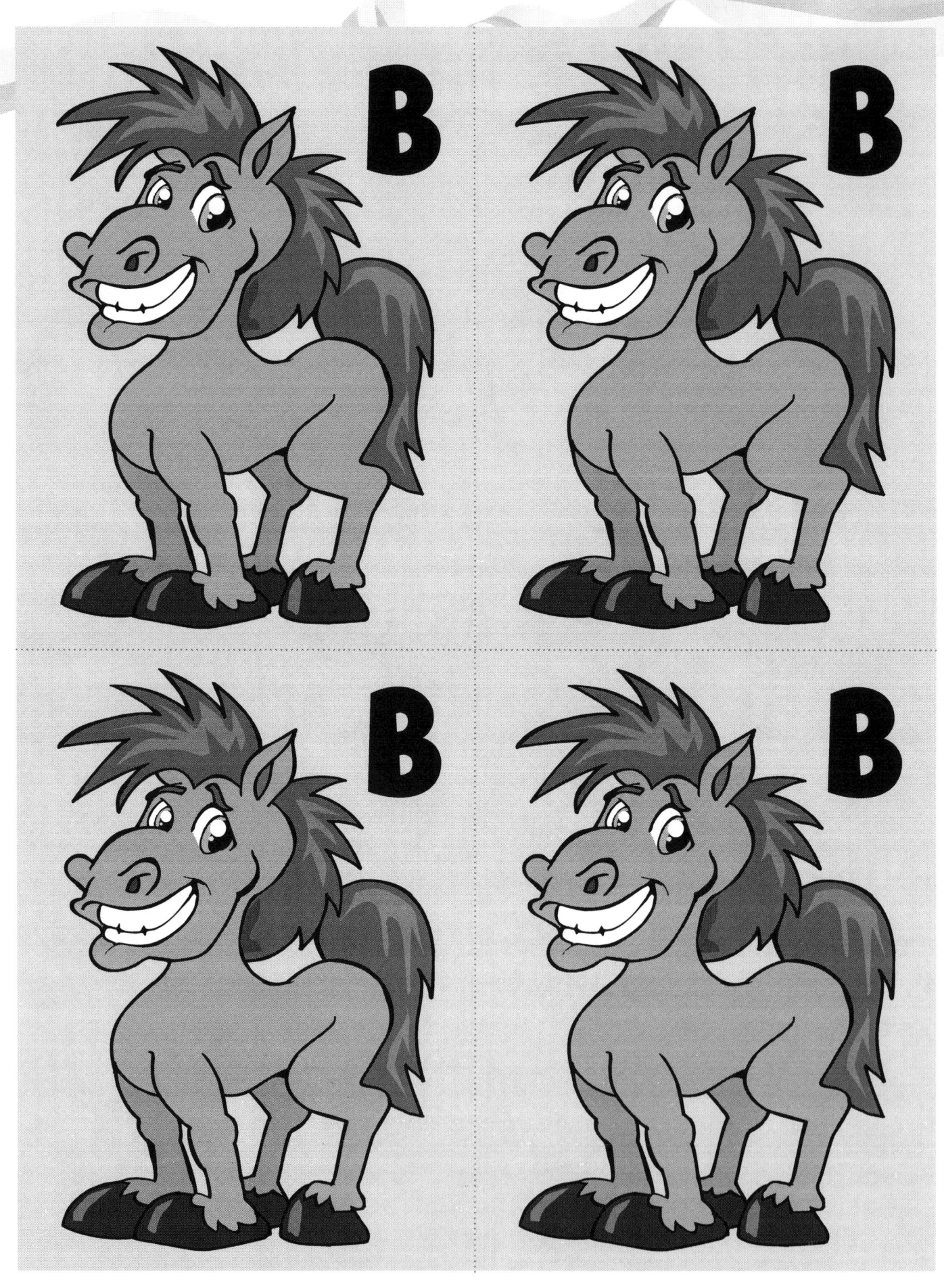

The original purchaser of *Parachutes and Ribbons and Scarves, Oh My!* (30/2626H) by Artie Almeida has permission to reproduce this page for use in his or her classroom setting. © 2011 Heritage Music Press, a division of The Lorenz Corporation.

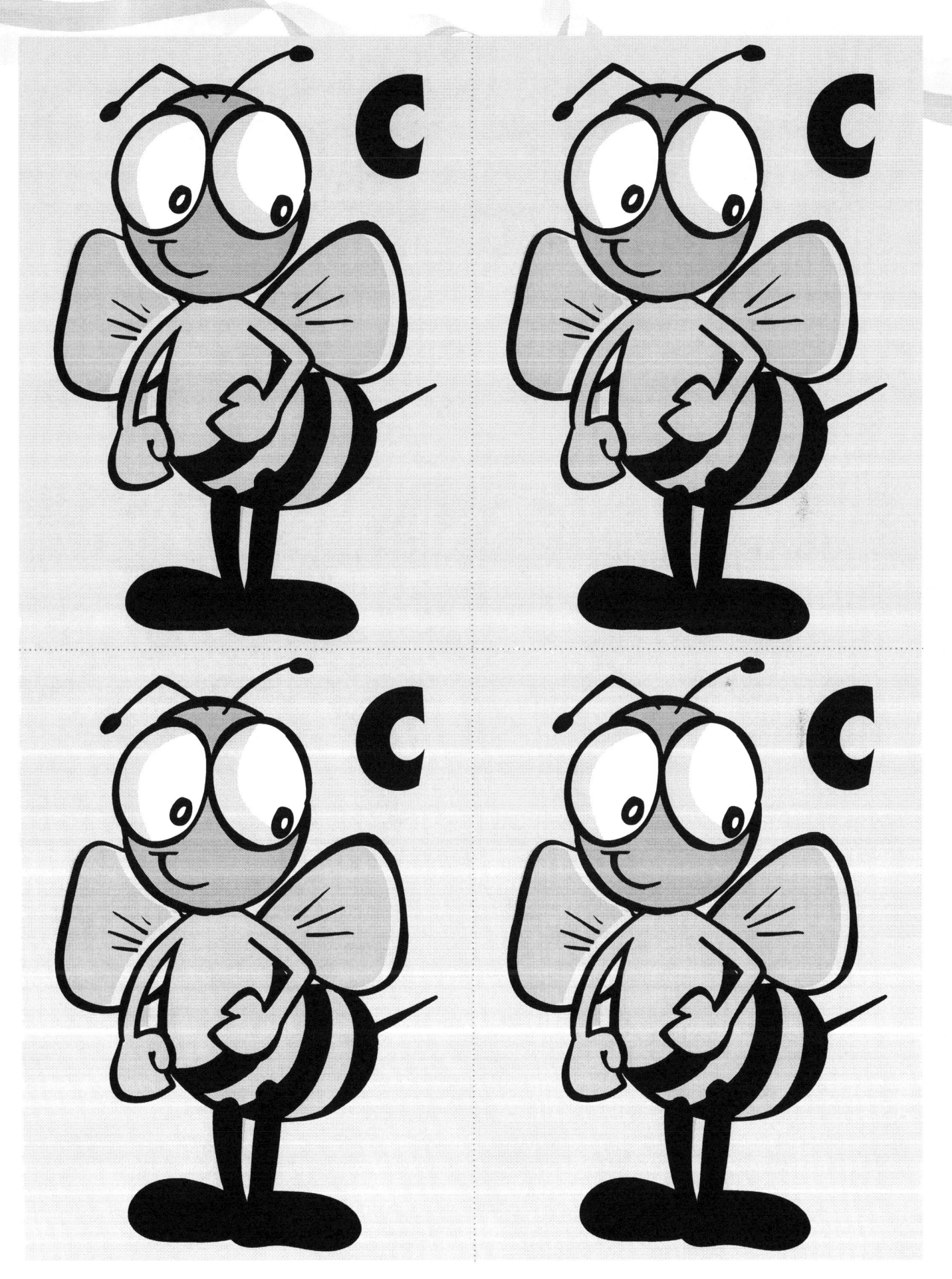

The original purchaser of *Parachutes and Ribbons and Scarves, Oh My!* (30/2626H) by Artie Almeida has permission to reproduce this page for use in his or her classroom setting. © 2011 Heritage Music Press, a division of The Lorenz Corporation.

61

CODA CODA

CODA CODA

Rondo alla Turca

Family Musical Moment
Today in music class we listened to *Rondo Alla Turca* composed by Wolfgang Amadeus Mozart. Our instructional goals included Form and Melodic Direction. We activated the lesson with Animal Responders. Share a musical moment with your child by listening to this exciting piece of music together.

Family Musical Moment
Today in music class we listened to *Rondo Alla Turca* composed by Wolfgang Amadeus Mozart. Our instructional goals included Form and Melodic Direction. We activated the lesson with Animal Responders. Share a musical moment with your child by listening to this exciting piece of music together.

Family Musical Moment
Today in music class we listened to *Rondo Alla Turca* composed by Wolfgang Amadeus Mozart. Our instructional goals included Form and Melodic Direction. We activated the lesson with Animal Responders. Share a musical moment with your child by listening to this exciting piece of music together.

Family Musical Moment
Today in music class we listened to *Rondo Alla Turca* composed by Wolfgang Amadeus Mozart. Our instructional goals included Form and Melodic Direction. We activated the lesson with Animal Responders. Share a musical moment with your child by listening to this exciting piece of music together.

Family Musical Moment
Today in music class we listened to *Rondo Alla Turca* composed by Wolfgang Amadeus Mozart. Our instructional goals included Form and Melodic Direction. We activated the lesson with Animal Responders. Share a musical moment with your child by listening to this exciting piece of music together.

FLAG ROUTINE

The Stars and Stripes Forever

By John Philip Sousa (1854–1932)

Suggested Grade Levels: 2–5

This exciting flag routine was created by Mrs. Tiffanie Pirro Brown, a fabulous young music educator who did her senior internship with me at Bear Lake Elementary in 2009. With her permission, I have modified it somewhat for use in my classes.

MATERIALS

Recording—Track 10
Small, handheld American flags, two per student
Picture of John Philip Sousa (see page 68)
Form Chart (see page 67)

INSTRUCTIONAL STEPS

1. Ask your students to define *patriotic song*. Explain that today's lesson will utilize a patriotic march—a band piece composed in honor of America.

2. Display a picture of John Philip Sousa. (I do this using my computer and projector.)

3. Share the following "Ten Tidbits" about John Philip Sousa:

    1. He lived from 1854–1932.
    2. His nickname was "The March King." Ask children why they think he had this nickname.
    3. He played the violin.
    4. He had perfect pitch, which means he could accurately hear every musical pitch in his head, and identify it.
    5. His father enlisted him in the Marines at age 13!
    6. His father did this to keep him from joining a circus band.
    7. John Philip Sousa served seven years in the Marine Band and played all the wind instruments. Ask your students to name some wind instruments.
    8. He organized his own band, and the Sousa Band was much beloved by Americans.
    9. He was famous for his invigorating and uplifting marches.
    10. He wrote 136 marches!

4. Discuss the form of this march. In basic terms it is Introduction/AABBCDCDC. The official march terminology would be valuable for your intermediate students to learn. It is listed on the next page.*

---

* A big thank you to our local wind-band expert, Mr. Michael Garasi, for confirming these terms!

The Stars and Stripes Forever

    Introduction
    First Strain (repeated)
    Second Strain (repeated)
    Trio
    Break Strain (Dogfight, so called because the two musical elements are arguing with each other)
    Trio (featuring the famous piccolo solo)
    Break Strain (Dogfight)
    Final Strain (piccolo solo returns at a *fortissimo* dynamic; ends with a stinger)

5. Demonstrate the various movements that are needed for this piece. I show my students:

    Flags crossed on chest
    Small figure eight with one hand, then both
    Large figure eights
    Tapping flags on the right side, then left
    Conducting while moving flags up and down
    Conducting to the right side, then left
    Windshield wipers above head
    Salutes down from right side of the students' foreheads
    "Drum taps" to right and left sides
    Shaking up high, and then shaking flag from high to low
    Marching while waving the flag up and down in front of the body
    Marching while waving the flag back and forth above the head
    Making large circles in front of the body
    Arms and flags raised up to create a "V" for the stinger at the end

6. Have your students spread out in the space. Distribute two flags to each student and allow them time to practice these movements. Lead your students through each move, if needed.

7. Perform the following routine, instructing your students to keep their eyes on you, listen for your verbal cues, and enjoy the music!*

    Introduction
    Two measures of rests, flags crossed on chest.

    First Strain and the repeat
    Move right arm above head and wave small figure eights to the beat. (16 beats)

    Move left arm above head and wave small figure eights to the beat. (16 beats)

    Move both arms above head and wave figure eights. (16 beats)

    Tap both flags to right side of body (4 beats), and then to left side (4 beats).

    Tap both flags to right side of body (4 beats), and then to left side (4 beats).

    Second Strain and the repeat
    Conduct with both hands from low to high (above the head) and back down using small motions. (8 beats up and 8 down)

---
*   I conduct this routine in reverse for the children. So when the directions indicate to put right arm up in the air, I mean the *student's* right arm. All directional words in these instructions are written from the student's viewpoint.

Repeat. (16 beats)

Conduct to right side of the body using large motions. (16 beats)

Conduct to left side of the body using large motions. (16 beats)

Trio
Use both flags to draw large, slow figure eights in front of the body. (32 beats)

Use both flags to wave "windshield wipers" above the head. (24 beats)

Finish the section with four salutes, matching the accents in the music.

Break Strain (Dogfight)
Hold flags out to the right side of the body and tap (like tapping a drum head) the two quarter notes that the full band plays after the trombone statement.

Do the same to the right side of body on next phrase (two eighth notes and a quarter note).

Repeat the tapping parts.

Move the right arm quickly above your head, and then bring it down, shaking it to the eighth-note pattern.

Move the left arm quickly above your head, and then bring it down, shaking it to the eighth-note pattern.

Move the right arm quickly above the head and shake it twice, matching the accents.

Move the left arm quickly above the head and shake it twice, matching the accents.

Wave both flags down from high to low. (8 beats)

Trio
March around room for 16 beats, while waving the flags up and down in front of body, alternating left, then right.

Continue marching while waving the flags back and forth above the head for 16 beats.

Continue marching while waving the flags up and down in front of the body for 16 beats, but turn and move back toward your starting position. March in place when you reach your starting position.*

March in place while waving the flags back and forth above the head for 8 beats.

Draw three large circles in front of the body, then place the flags crossed on the chest on the final note.

Break Strain (Dogfight) repeats
Repeat the movements as outlined for the first Break Strain.

Final Strain
Repeat the Trio movements as given above, but throw both of the arms into air in a "V" formation on the stinger! Freeze in this final pose.

8. Give your students a Family Musical Moment note (found on page 69) as they leave so they can find the music online.

---

* I have found that it is a little less chaotic at the end if I can get all students back into their starting position, where everyone is facing me for the cues to finish the piece, but this is optional. If you wish, you can have students freeze for the upcoming large circles and salutes.

Form Chart: The Stars and Stripes Forever

Introduction

First Strain (repeated)

Second Strain (repeated)

Trio

Break Strain (Dogfight)

Trio

Break Strain (Dogfight)

Final Strain, with Stinger!

John Philip Sousa (1854–1932)

The Stars and Stripes Forever

Family Musical Moment
Today in music class we listened to a patriotic march called *The Stars and Stripes Forever* composed by John Philip Sousa. We activated the experience with a flag routine. The instructional focus included Steady Beat and Form. Share a musical moment with your child by listening to this exciting piece of music together.

Family Musical Moment
Today in music class we listened to a patriotic march called *The Stars and Stripes Forever* composed by John Philip Sousa. We activated the experience with a flag routine. The instructional focus included Steady Beat and Form. Share a musical moment with your child by listening to this exciting piece of music together.

Family Musical Moment
Today in music class we listened to a patriotic march called *The Stars and Stripes Forever* composed by John Philip Sousa. We activated the experience with a flag routine. The instructional focus included Steady Beat and Form. Share a musical moment with your child by listening to this exciting piece of music together.

Family Musical Moment
Today in music class we listened to a patriotic march called *The Stars and Stripes Forever* composed by John Philip Sousa. We activated the experience with a flag routine. The instructional focus included Steady Beat and Form. Share a musical moment with your child by listening to this exciting piece of music together.

Family Musical Moment
Today in music class we listened to a patriotic march called *The Stars and Stripes Forever* composed by John Philip Sousa. We activated the experience with a flag routine. The instructional focus included Steady Beat and Form. Share a musical moment with your child by listening to this exciting piece of music together.

A Plastic Cup Routine

El Capitan

By John Philip Sousa (1854–1932)

Suggested Grade Levels: 3–5

> I created this routine on September 12, 2001 to add an American patriotic march to my lessons in honor of the lost souls of September 11th. We sang patriotic songs and did this cup routine. My students have enjoyed this march over the years, and always have fun with the challenge of the passing game.

MATERIALS

Recording—Track 11
Red, white, and blue plastic cups*
Picture of El Capitan (see page 74)

INSTRUCTIONAL STEPS

1. Ask your students to define "patriotic song." Explain that today's lesson will utilize a patriotic march—a band piece composed in honor of America. Ask your students if they think marching band music will have words (lyrics). (No, it won't, because people in a marching band play instruments.)

2. Display a picture of the mountain El Capitan. It is most striking to see a color photograph, so you can use a computer and projector, with a picture from the internet or the one provided with the downloadable files.

3. Share the following five fun facts about El Capitan:

    1. It is a 3,000 foot tall granite rock formation located in Yosemite National Park.

    2. El Capitan means "The Captain" or "The Chief."

    3. It was carved by glaciers.

    4. It is a favorite of rock climbers from around the world.

    5. One portion of the monolith is called the nose!

---

*   Having trouble finding white plastic cups? Try a party store! That's where I get mine.

El Capitan

4. Discuss the form of this march. The form below, which uses march-specific vocabulary, is valuable for your intermediate students to learn.* If you're using this lesson with primary-aged children, you might prefer to describe the form as Introduction/AABBCC/Interlude/DD.

   Introduction
   First Strain (repeated)
   Second Strain (repeated)
   Trio (repeated)
   Episode
   Last Strain (repeated)
   Stinger

5. During the first listening experience, focus on a specific musical item in each section. I encourage the children to listen for the following musical details:

   Introduction: *Forte*, bold start, four measures long
   First Strain: Melody in wind instruments, with accents enhanced by percussion, $\frac{6}{8}$ time
   Second Strain: Listen for the *crescendos* that make this section exciting
   Trio: The music modulates to a higher key and the meter changes to $\frac{2}{4}$
   Episode: An exciting conversation among the brass family, promising a powerful ending to the piece
   Last Strain: Soft woodwinds first time through, and then the brasses enter on the repeat and "pull out all the stops!"
   Stinger: A strong, last note ends the piece

6. Distribute two plastic cups (both in the same color) to each student. I either alternate red, white, and blue amongst the students, or group the colors together so that each color is designated to one third of the circle.

7. Practice each of the cup movements outlined below before starting the music. Make sure the spacing is such that the children can comfortably tap the bottoms of their cups against the cup bottoms of each of their neighbors.

   Starting position
   Hold a cup in each hand as you would to drink from it, with cups resting on your legs.

   Introduction
   Hold cups still on legs during the two measures of rests.

   First Strain
   Tap the bottom of the cup twice on floor, then tap the cup bottoms against each other twice, all to a quarter-note pulse. Do four sets of this pattern. (You might provide your students with a cue such as, "Floor, floor, together, together" or "Floor, floor, tap, tap.")

   Scrape the sides of the cups against each other to a half-note pulse four times, then seven quarter-note scrapes. Rest for a beat at the end of the seven quarter-note scrapes. (You might use the following cue phrase, "Scrape—two, three, four. One, two, three, four, five, six, seven, rest." You can hear me say this in the video demo.)

   Repeat the entire first-strain pattern, but on the last quarter note, place the cup in your non-dominant hand upside-down on the floor, approximately twelve inches in front of your body.

---
* My thanks to Michael Garasi, our local wind-band expert, for verifying the march-form terms.

Second Strain
Tap your cup bottom on the palm of your empty hand four times, and then toss the cup into the air. The toss completes the *crescendo* in the music! Then, reach forward and tap your cup bottom on the upside-down cup seven times. Repeat this entire pattern of tapping hand, tossing, and then tapping the upturned cup four times. At the end, place the cup on the ground upright!

Trio
Tell the children to put their dominant hand in the air over their cup, and to say what you say and do what you do, but to NOT touch their cup until you direct them to. Speak the words "Tap, tap, pass" eight times while miming the pattern with the children. Then, instruct the children to pick up the cup. Speak the direction, "Ready! Here we go!" and begin the actual passing game for eight sets, which will be sixteen measures of music. (These directions may seem complex, but in watching the video, you will see that the pattern is relatively easy for the children.)

Episode (Interlude)
To prepare for the final strain, give the following verbal directions: "Pick up your cups. Turn them upright. Get ready for two taps on the floor, then two against your neighbor. Here we go!" Time these spoken directions so that they are completed just before the Last Strain begins.

Last Strain
Tap the cup bottoms together twice with the quarter-note pulse, then reach out to sides and tap your neighbors' cup bottoms twice. Do this eight times. On the repeat, the bottoms-together rhythm changes from the quarter-note pulse to a ti-ti-ta pattern. Students still tap their neighbors' cup bottoms twice. Repeat this entire pattern seven times. (If this seems confusing, remember this cup routine is demonstrated on the video.)

In the final measure have your student "stack 'em and wear 'em" by placing one cup inside the other, and then setting the cups on their heads like a little hat (holding it there with one hand). On the stinger, students should extend their other hand dramatically out in front of their bodies. We always reward ourselves with a round of "cup applause" at the end!

8. Give your students a Family Musical Moment note (found on page 75) as they leave so they can find the music online.

Form Chart: El Capitan

Introduction

First Strain (repeated)

Second Strain (repeated)

Trio (repeated)

Episode

Last Strain (repeated)

Stinger

El Capitan

The original purchaser of *Parachutes and Ribbons and Scarves, Oh My!* (30/2626H) by Artie Almeida has permission to reproduce this page for use in his or her classroom setting. This image of El Capitan provided by Wikimedia user Poppy. The original is available at: http://commons.wikimedia.org/wiki/File:El_Capitan_1.jpg. The image and the page that contains it are licensed under the Creative Commons Attribution-Share Alike 3.0 Unported license. http://creativecommons.org/licenses/by-sa/3.0/deed.en

El Capitan

Family Musical Moment
Today in music class we listened to a patriotic march called *El Capitan* composed by John Philip Sousa. We activated the experience with a cup passing game. The instructional focus included Steady Beat and Form. Share a musical moment with your child by listening to this exciting piece of music together.

Family Musical Moment
Today in music class we listened to a patriotic march called *El Capitan* composed by John Philip Sousa. We activated the experience with a cup passing game. The instructional focus included Steady Beat and Form. Share a musical moment with your child by listening to this exciting piece of music together.

Family Musical Moment
Today in music class we listened to a patriotic march called *El Capitan* composed by John Philip Sousa. We activated the experience with a cup passing game. The instructional focus included Steady Beat and Form. Share a musical moment with your child by listening to this exciting piece of music together.

Family Musical Moment
Today in music class we listened to a patriotic march called *El Capitan* composed by John Philip Sousa. We activated the experience with a cup passing game. The instructional focus included Steady Beat and Form. Share a musical moment with your child by listening to this exciting piece of music together.

Family Musical Moment
Today in music class we listened to a patriotic march called *El Capitan* composed by John Philip Sousa. We activated the experience with a cup passing game. The instructional focus included Steady Beat and Form. Share a musical moment with your child by listening to this exciting piece of music together.

Experiencing Tempo and Dynamics with Kickballs and Guiros

"In the Hall of the Mountain King" from the *Peer Gynt Suite No. 1*

By Edvard Grieg (1843–1907)

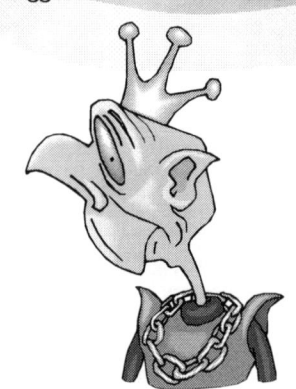

This piece is always a big hit with the children. They definitely understand the terms accelerando *and* crescendo *by the time the lesson is done!*

I borrow kickballs from my coaching staff. They usually let me borrow the air compressor for the week too so that, as the kickballs lose air, I can refill them slightly so that they bounce well on the carpeting. The kickballs are large enough, and soft enough, to be grabbed and controlled easily. A few will still get away though, as you'll see in our video.

Materials

Recording—Track 12
Kickballs (enough for half of the class)
Guiros (enough for half of the class)
Crescendo and *Accelerando* Flash Cards (see pages 79 and 80)

Instructional Steps

1. Have your students find Norway on a map. Ask the children if they know any facts about the country.

2. Share the following five fun facts about Norway:

    1. Over half of Norway is covered by mountains.
    2. Norway has a large population of reindeer.
    3. Norway has many beautiful fjords. Fjords are narrow inlets of the sea, between steep cliffs.
    4. Norwegians love to ski! There is a popular expression that "Norwegians are born with skis."
    5. Norway is called "The Land of the Midnight Sun." During part of the summer, the sun is out both day and night.

3. Display the *Crescendo* and *Accelerando* flash cards. Define the terms and encourage the children to listen to how these two expressive qualities make this music one of the most exciting and suspenseful pieces ever written.

"In the Hall of the Mountain King" from the Peer Gynt Suite No. 1

4. With your students seated, prepare the following dramatic storytelling or find/create your own version.*

   Once there was a naughty boy named Peer Gynt. He was a practical joker who kidnapped a bride from her own wedding and abandoned her on a mountainside. The wedding guests were very angry and started searching for Peer, who hid behind some bushes in front of a cave. Suddenly, he was snatched into the cave by trolls and brought to a disgusting-looking (and smelly!) large, green troll—the Mountain King. The king decided that Peer should wed his lovely (yeah, right!) daughter and become a troll himself.

   As the wedding planning begins and the hall is filled with trolls decorating, cooking, and dressing the beautiful bride, Peer finds his opportunity to sneak away. *(Begin playing the recording.)* He begins tiptoeing through a tunnel, which branches off from the main hall, and continues deeper and deeper into the mountain. The tunnel grows smaller and smaller, until Peer is almost on his hands and knees trying to escape. He hears the click-clack of little troll claws behind him and realizes that all of the trolls are giving chase. With his heart pounding, Peer goes even faster, racing through a maze of tunnels, hoping to find his way out of the mountain. *(I draw out this part of the story with twists and turns in the tunneling, the clanking of the trolls' spears against the walls, etc. I get louder and louder, with more and more suspense in my voice.)*

   The mountain suddenly shakes twice from a powerful earthquake, then shakes twice again. Finally the mountain gives three great shakes and crashes down in a heap. Just before the final three shakes, Peer sees a light at the end of the tunnel! Could it be the outside and safety? He throws himself toward the light…

   Finish listening to the recording. After the final chord sounds, conclude the story. I say, "And the good news is that Peer went flying right out the side of the mountain to safety—just before it collapsed! And all of the trolls were squashed flatter than flitters!"

5. Following the story, divide your class into two groups: half will do the kickball-bouncing routine, while the other half plays guiros to the beat. Pick a very responsible, good listener to be the student leader of the guiro group.

6. Arrange the students in the guiro group in a line off to one side, facing their student leader. Instruct them to start with very small, soft scrapes. They will increase the size and the volume of the scrapes as the piece intensifies. Be careful that they do not get too loud too soon (this is always a problem with my classes). Ask the children to keep their eyes on the student leader—who is keeping his/her eyes on you—to be sure that they are playing exactly on the beat to which you are bouncing the ball. When the earthquake begins, the guiro players must make very large scrapes on each shake of the mountain, and then roll (rapid scraping back and forth) while the kickball kids do a turn. On the final phrase the guiros roll, then play the final note loudly, then freeze.

---

*   I always introduce the music with this storytelling. The children are riveted! Mouths open, eyes wide, completely silent. Woohoo! So few children these days have heard any dramatic storytelling, the minute we finish they are begging to hear it again. They really love it! You can find numerous versions of this story online if the outline here doesn't suit you. I really jazz it up with gross details of the troll's appearance, Peer's astonishment when smelly little creatures grab him by the ankles and drag him back into the mountain, the sweat dripping off him as he scrambles through the tunnels, his regret over being so naughty and playing practical jokes on people, etc. I used to teach this lesson in kindergarten, first, and second grades, but I was afraid that those children would be scared that night at home, even though I told a much tamer version to the primary grades. So I teach this lesson only to students in the intermediate grades now.

7. Instruct the students in the kickball group to watch you and do what you do. Perform the following routine with the kickball:

During the first four measures of music, internalize the beat through subtle movements such as swaying or bouncing. In the fifth measure, begin bouncing the ball to the beat.

After every eight measures, change from bouncing the kickball on the floor to tossing it hand-to-hand in the air. If this tossing is too challenging for the small hands, they can just pass it back and forth between hands.

At the earthquake, bounce the ball two times, then hold it above the head and turn in a circle.

Repeat the motion to the music again.

On the final three shakes, bounce the ball three times, wave it back and forth above the head, and finish with a large bounce on the final note.

Catch the ball in one hand and freeze in that final pose.

8. Exchange roles/instruments and repeat the activity so that all students get to experience both activities.

9. Give your students a Family Musical Moment note as they leave so they can find the music online.

Family Musical Moment

Today in music class we listened to "In the Hall of the Mountain King" from the *Peer Gynt Suite* composed by Edvard Grieg. We activated the experience with kickballs and guiros. The instructional focus included Tempo (*accelerando*) and Dynamics (*crescendo*). Share a musical moment with your child by listening to this exciting piece of music together.

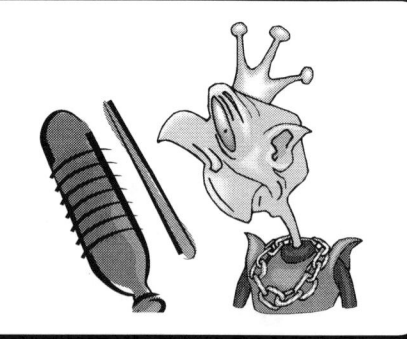

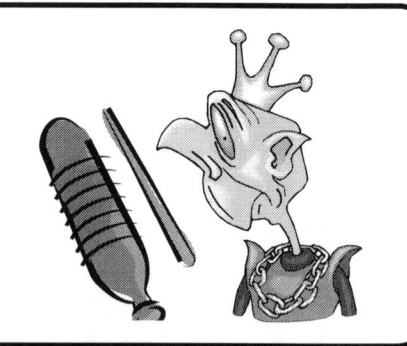

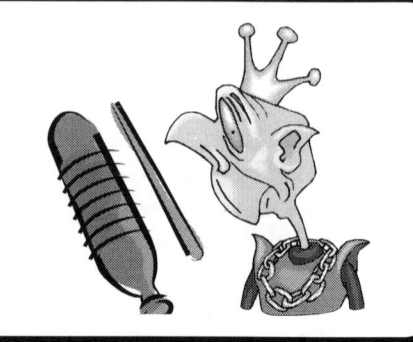

Family Musical Moment

Today in music class we listened to "In the Hall of the Mountain King" from the *Peer Gynt Suite* composed by Edvard Grieg. We activated the experience with kickballs and guiros. The instructional focus included Tempo (*accelerando*) and Dynamics (*crescendo*). Share a musical moment with your child by listening to this exciting piece of music together.

Family Musical Moment

Today in music class we listened to "In the Hall of the Mountain King" from the *Peer Gynt Suite* composed by Edvard Grieg. We activated the experience with kickballs and guiros. The instructional focus included Tempo (*accelerando*) and Dynamics (*crescendo*). Share a musical moment with your child by listening to this exciting piece of music together.

Accelerando

The original purchaser of *Parachutes and Ribbons and Scarves, Oh My!* (30/2626H) by Artie Almeida has permission to reproduce this page for use in his or her classroom setting. © 2011 Heritage Music Press, a division of The Lorenz Corporation.

Crescendo

The original purchaser of *Parachutes and Ribbons and Scarves, Oh My!* (30/2626H) by Artie Almeida has permission to reproduce this page for use in his or her classroom setting. © 2011 Heritage Music Press, a division of The Lorenz Corporation.